Straight Talk for Teenage Girls

By

Annette Fuson

ISBN: 1-4033-3273-8 (ebook)
ISBN: 1-4033-3274-6 (Paperback)

Library of Congress Control Number: 2002093966

This book is printed on acid free paper.

Printed in the United States of America
Bloomington, IN

1stBooks - rev. 08/13/02

This book is dedicated to the thousands of teenage girls who have touched my life:

Central Dauphin High School
Harrisburg, PA
Harrison Township School
Harrison, IN
Storer Middle School
Muncie, IN
My wonderful daughter,
Sheree Fuson Bizzell
My granddaughter Michelle Bizzell,
who will someday soon be a teenager

Introduction

I have been teaching teenage girls for nearly 25 years. All the changes in teenage girls' lives make them so confused, afraid and frustrated. They silently plead for help. What they long for is someone to listen to them and give them love, understanding and guidance so they can make good decisions. Too often, parents are busy working two jobs, are divorced or have blended families and are dealing with their own pressures. A teenage girl, with hormones raging, is not the easiest person to confront. Everyone means well, it is just that circumstances and personalities get things blown out of proportion.

This book is a small synopsis of what I taught teenage girls to help them through this tough part of their life. They need an enormous amount of strokes, hints, information, ideas and encouragement during these years. It is in everyone's best interest, for now and the future, that they all become happy, well-rounded adults with a minimum of problems along the way. To this end is my purpose.

Table of Contents

Chapter 1

Teen Years

Jodi, 14, is so worried! All her friends' bodies are so curvy and her body hasn't changed a bit. She still looks like a boy. "What is wrong with me?" "Will I look like this forever?" She is upset because people laugh and make fun of her. She finds herself crying so many times for no reason. Jodi still likes to ride her bike and play baseball, but her friends want to sit, talk about boys and listen to music. She is so confused. "What are these teen years all about?" she wonders. "What is going to happen to me?"

Your teen years will be some of the best times of your life! You'll learn to do so many new things, make some great friendships and have fabulous experiences that are free from the responsibilities of adulthood. It is a time to be and to become. It is a time of innocence and challenges. So don't forget to enjoy this time. During these last years of school you can find out what you really enjoy. Enter the science club, join the debate team, sing in the choir, play an instrument, join the art club, be in a play, get on a team sport. Don't be afraid to try out new activities. You may find a lifelong enjoyment or hobby. You'll also meet lots of new friends this way. Life will be what YOU make it.

However, don't be fooled, for these years will also hand you some of the worst times of your life. You are traveling toward adulthood, and the road is full of bumps. You will come face to face with some hard choices that will affect the rest of your life. Smoking, drinking, drugs, sex...all lurking to see what you will do and how you will handle it. Just remember, <u>everyone</u> goes through these times and you will make it too. This book is written to help you make some choices and to give you guidance as you go. As you mature, decisions become harder because the choices are harder and more involved. People tend to put you on the spot and make you feel guilty or belittled. Friends will call you a baby if you don't want to try things. You want their friendship, so you compromise your own values to do what they want...not what you want. Values are what are important to you. Think for a minute. What do you value? Family, friends, honesty, health, fun, looks, money, possessions, religion, dependability, trust, freedom. Values come from your family upbringing, religion, teachers, people around you, television, music, etc. Things you are taught, beliefs of right from wrong, or things you live by. They are usually very deep in your heart and you sometimes don't know you have them until someone "tests" you by wanting you to do something you don't believe is right.

It is very important, as teenagers, to learn to make "right" choices. Choices that won't put you in a bad situation, won't hurt you or hurt your future, won't get you in trouble with the law or your parents. Right choices, not regrettable mistakes. THINK before you make choices:

How do I feel about it? (not how others feel)

What will happen if I do it? If I don't do it?

What bad could happen to me? Could I handle it?

How will the choice affect my future?

Am I being pressured?

How will I feel about it tomorrow?

You can always say things like:

"I'm not ready to try that yet."

"Maybe another time."

"I don't feel like that now."

"Not now, thanks."

"Sorry, I can't now."

"My folks would kill me!"

"I can't, I'm in training for_____."

If you are 13-15 years old, your teen years are in the beginning stages. Your body is changing. Curves are starting, you're growing taller, your period has started and your emotions go up and down like a yo-yo. You'll feel like a child one moment and someone completely different the next. Some days you'll want to crawl into a shell and other times scream at the world. You'll change your looks and ideas like a chameleon. That's what teens do. Find the chapters here that will help guide you toward the lovely young lady you are going to become.

If you are 16-18 years old, you've made it to sweet 16. Now come the hard choices and decisions. You're still changing, but slowly becoming surer of yourself. You've begun to wonder what you'll do with your life. Will you get a job, go on to college or trade school, get married and have children? Decisions about smoking, drinking, drugs and sex will all rise to greet you. You'll have more freedom, get to drive, stay out later, choose your friends and make life decisions. Hopefully, you're getting involved in plays, musicals, sports, clubs, groups and so many new and different activities. That means making new friends and having new challenges. This is the time in your life to mold your personality and shape your future.

The chapters that are here for you will give you ideas and guidance toward the graceful and confident young adult you are becoming.

Your "job" is to become the best person you can be. Your teen years are when you are going through the building stage. You'll be trying to find out who you are and what you want to become. It is trial and error. It will be bumpy, but it will be fun too. As you experience both good and bad, remember to ask yourself: **"Is this what's best for ME?"**…and you will do well.

Chapter 2

Knowing & Liking Yourself

Kayla, 15, is much shorter than all her friends. She feels like they think she's a little kid. Some people call her half-pint or shortie to tease her. She makes good grades, but she doesn't know how to wear make up or fix her hair. She has no interest in those things. Kayla feels like she doesn't fit in. She loves babysitting because she likes reading stories and playing games with little kids. They like being with her, too. Kayla keeps wondering, "Why can't I be like everyone else? Why am I so different?"

Do you know that of all the millions of people in the world, there is only ONE person like you? That seems unbelievable, but it is true. There is only one you. When there is only one of anything, it is very rare and precious. You are one of a kind; that's awesome.

Who are you? Get a pencil and paper and let's see who you are. Stop! Don't write down "I'm nobody". You are not a blank piece of paper. Let's start with you're a girl, a teen, a person. What else? Add to the list.

Now, let's consider what you like about your looks. No, don't say "nothing." Look closely. Do you have long eyelashes, big eyes, a cute nose, small ears, a nicely shaped mouth, straight teeth, beautiful hair, long nails, high cheek bones? You probably have at least two or three. What talents do you have? Are you musical? Do you sing well or play an instrument? Are you artistic, good at a sport, good at math or English? Can you write poetry? Are you good with children, pets, old people or babies? Maybe you are a good cook or a gardener or perhaps you are good at crafts, good with make-up, hair or nails. Do you have a sense of humor? Can you make people laugh? Are you fun to be around? Are you honest, dependable, responsible? Can you keep a secret? Are you on time? Can you be trusted?

Make your own list. You'll be amazed at the wonderful things you find out about yourself. Ask others who know you what they see that you are good at. What are your interests? Is there something you'd like to do as a hobby? If so, take lessons to get better, talk to people who are good at it and ask for hints to help you. Set a goal. Practice, practice, practice. Join a class to learn more about it. No one is born good at something: it is learned. So you can learn it, too.

Don't look at what you dislike about yourself. That will only make you depressed. Anyway, if it is your looks, you can't do a lot about that, move on and accept that you are short, or your feet are too big, etc. Look at the things you **can** change and work on those. No one is good at everything. We all have some things we are better at than other people. Then there are things we are not good at, at all. That's normal.

Now that you've looked at things about yourself, it is essential that you begin to like some of those things. Force

9

yourself, if need be. Make a small sign that says "I like myself" or "I'm an important person". Put it in your room where you can see it every day. Read it each day. Then look in the mirror and say something good to yourself that's true. Like; "you have pretty hair", "your smile is great", "you are funny", "I like your eyes." If you do this every day, after awhile you will believe it and begin to feel better about yourself. If you are a young teenager, think of an older teen that you think is beautiful. Then find her in an old yearbook when she was 10 or 12 years old. You'll be amazed at the change! That will give you hope. Some of the most beautiful swans were ugly ducklings. This is a fact of life.

If you were to ask the most beautiful, talented girl you know if she is pleased with herself, you'd be shocked at her answer. She may be a cheerleader, make good grades, have lots of friends, go with a cute guy; but she will not be completely happy with herself. Everyone finds fault with themselves and are not pleased with who they are. Maybe they expect perfection, but there is no such thing. NO TEEN IS COMPLETELY HAPPY WITH WHO THEY ARE. So stop bellyaching. It is time to take a real look at who and what you are and accept it happily.

Everyone needs self-esteem. Having self-esteem can help you make it through hard times. The trouble is you can't buy it, steal it or borrow it. You must develop it. It is important. Because people with self-esteem are less likely to be talked into things they don't want to do. You have already started getting it by seeing what you like about yourself and what you are good at. Now let's go farther. What are some things you'd like to try? What have you put off? Choose something you've been meaning to do. It can be taking a class, cleaning your room, finishing something you started, planting some flowers, giving your pet a bath, learning a new dance or doing a craft. Something simple. Now find the time. Make a plan and start it. You will feel so good after you accomplish it. (Don't let others put you down with their nasty remarks, either.)

Have you always wanted to learn to sew, make a craft, take guitar lessons, learn to dive, write poetry, learn to bowl or skate, or play tennis or chess? You fill in the blank. "I always wanted to_____." Ok, DO IT! Go to the library and get some books to see about it. See if a class is offered at a college nearby. Are there people in your area who do this? Talk to people you know who are good at this. Make a plan to start. Now, do it. Every time you finally do something you've wanted to do, you'll feel great for trying it...even if you weren't a pro at it. These things help you feel good about yourself.

You can change the way you feel about yourself by changing the way you act. Look at habits that lead you to a negative self-image. Change the situations that leave you feeling down. When you think negative thoughts, turn them around and say to yourself, "They don't really know me". "I am good at _____." "I'm a good friend, and Sally likes me" etc... Think and act in a way that makes you feel you are worth something. Think about that area in your life - school, friends, family - that you feel insecure or frustrated about. What can you do about it? It is really up to you and in your mind. **PEOPLE CAN'T MAKE YOU FEEL BAD WITHOUT YOUR PERMISSION!**

You also must believe in yourself…You may not be around people who tell you how good you are. If instead, you have people who always tell you that you "can't do" or "you're not good" etc… then you need to put on that coat of armor so what they say can't get to you. Some people say nasty things to you because they are jealous. They have a low self-esteem, and therefore feel better when they can tear other people down. Don't let them do this to you. Keep telling yourself "you can do it", "you are worthwhile!" It really only matters what you think, not others. Start being around people who make you feel good, not bad.

The following are certain things that <u>all</u> people have in common. Look at them and realize you are not alone in your feelings.

1. **No one is perfect**… Remember when you feel down, it is because something doesn't go right for you.

2. **We are ALL human beings with feelings**…Human beings make mistakes and get upset.

3. **We are all unique**…We're different and that's good.

4. **Everyone has a right to an opinion**…Opinions are not right or wrong, just what you think.

5. **Everyone needs to feel important**…It doesn't matter who you are.

6. **We all come from different backgrounds and cultures**…Ideas will be different, not right or wrong.

7. **We have different values**...Because we are raised by different people.

8. **No one likes to be put down or belittled**...So think before you speak.

9. **No one can make you feel sad, mad, glad**...You choose how you feel.

10. **We only have control over ourselves**...We can NOT control others.

How well do you like yourself? Take this little test on the following pages and start looking at yourself in a whole new light. After you take the test, concentrate on those traits that you checked 3's or 4's on. These are wonderful things to feel about yourself. Be glad you have some. Now begin to keep a positive attitude about yourself. After all, if you don't like yourself, how can you expect others to like you? Keep in mind, **"What is best for ME?"**

HOW WELL DO YOU LIKE YOURSELF?

Put the number in the blank that best tells your feelings.

4 - very true

3 - mostly true

2 - partly true

1 - hardly true

0 - not true

_____ I enjoy waking up in the morning

_____ I'm usually in a good mood

_____ Most people like me

_____ When I look in the mirror, I like what I see

_____ If I were a boy, I'd find me attractive

_____ I'm smart

_____ I enjoy school

_____ There aren't many things about me I'm ashamed of

_____ I have some good friends

_____ I have plenty of energy

_____ I'm basically happy

_____ I can laugh at myself

_____ I have a hobby or interest

_____ I'm an interesting person

_____ I can make decisions

_____ I lead an interesting life

_____ I'm still growing & changing

_____ People care about me

_____ There's no one quite like me

_____There is only a little I'd change about my looks

_____I'm a kind person

_____I'm pretty happy with my life

_____People I care about value my opinions

_____I'm not afraid to talk to people

_____I enjoy being with my friends

_____I feel comfortable talking to my friends

_____I can make my life whatever I want it

_____I have an idea what I want to do as an adult

_____My life has fun in it

_____I like where I live

Add them up.

96 or above Congratulations! You have a very positive outlook about yourself.

72 - 95 You are a lucky person who likes herself.

48 - 71 You have mixed feelings and may be paying more attention to your weaknesses than your strengths.

Below 47 You are not happy with yourself. You need to talk with an adult about your self-concept.

Look at your 3's & 4's - They are your strong points.

Look at 1's & 0's - Here is where you need work. How can you change them?

Chapter 3

Dealing with Problems

Christi, 13, is having parent problems. Her mother and dad are divorced and her dad remarried. She is to spend every other weekend with him. Christi doesn't want to go that often because she always has to baby-sit his wife's two children, ages 5 and 8. She would really like to spend time alone with her dad, but she never gets to do that. Her mother says she **must** go and quit complaining. Christi feels used and doesn't think her dad cares about her feelings. She keeps dreaming, "I want to do what I want. How can I make that happen?"

Everyone has problems. Their problems are just different. The first thing in handling problems is to stop thinking negatively about them. Think of them as challenges, something you can deal with and do something about. Problems seem harder when you don't have experience dealing with them. It is something learned. You start with choices and decisions. You've been making decisions daily for many years. (What to wear and eat, when to do chores, what subject to take in school, choosing friends, etc.) Dealing with each challenge you have three choices: Accept it, cope with it or take action.

1. **ACCEPT IT** - This is what you do when you can't change it. There isn't anything you can do about it. For example:

   WEATHER - It's too hot, below zero, snowing or raining. You must get your mind off of it because you have no control over it.

   TOO SHORT/TALL - You have no control over your height. You may not like what you are, but you can't do anything about it - accept it. You can dress to look taller or shorter, but you can't change your height. The same is true about the size of your feet, ears, nose, bust, or lips. You must change your attitude so you can accept the way you are. Concentrate on things you can control. So when a problem arises, think "Can I do anything about it?" If not, accept it and go on.

2. **COPE** - You can't change these, but you can change the way you feel about them or develop ways to deal with them. For example: you can't change other people (parents, brother/sister, teacher, friends). You have no control over other people, but you can change the way YOU think about them. YOU CONTROL HOW YOU FEEL AND REACT TO OTHERS. You can ignore them, stay away from them. Look at their good points. Don't look at what upsets you. See life from their point of view. Learn why they act that way. Try to understand where they are coming from. Then learn ways to change

18

how you feel about them. Here are some problems and ways you can cope with them:

KIDS CALL YOU NAMES, or make fun of you. - You have no control over other people and what they do. You have to cope - find ways to deal with it. Why are they doing it? They are probably jealous of you. (You are prettier or smarter) People tend to put others down to make themselves feel better. They hope to upset you or make you mad, that's how they feel better. Ignore them as best you can. Stay away from them. Try to see life from their point of view, understanding why others do things. That will usually take the bad taste away. You end up feeling sorry for them. When you can learn ways to change how you feel about them, then you win and you're coping.

BROTHER TEASES YOU - ask yourself "why?" Is it to make you mad so you'll scream at him? Because he has to make you feel bad so he will feel better, bigger or more important? So mother will punish you, thinking you caused it? Okay, you know he is going to do it. Act like it doesn't bother you. Ignore him, like he isn't there. Treat him so sweet. Compliment him, ask his opinion of something or make him cookies, etc. Treat him as an equal. People can't continue hurting others when their victims treat them well or act as if they don't care.

MOTHER TELLING YOU WHAT TO DO - Mother nagging. Again, "why"? Because she loves you and wants to make sure you remember to do well? Because you forgot? Because she is a perfectionist? Is it a habit, or does she do this to everyone? Try talking to her. Such as, "Mother, I notice you remind me to do everything. This isn't helping me to become more independent and grown-up. Could we try an experiment? You list the things that worry you that you think I'll forget. Give me a week to work on doing them on my own. If you remind me, I'll put my finger on my nose to let you know not to help, okay?"

You might notice what things she reminds you to do that upsets you. Make a list and set a time frame to help you remember to do them before she reminds you. Try to be more organized. Get a laundry basket to put your dirty clothes in, hang up your clothes. Put your schoolbooks, etc. in a special place. Get a big wastebasket for your trash. Putting things away immediately keeps your room looking neat. See if cleaning your room once a week would make her happy.

TIME - Everyone has twenty-four hours in a day. It is how you manage and organize your time that will help you deal with it. You can't change the amount of time, you can only learn to manage it better. Make a plan. List what you have to do. Get a book that gives you a daily schedule. Get a calendar to keep track of your activities. Put it where you can see it daily. Check it regularly.

3. **ACTION** - These are problems you CAN CHANGE. You do have control over them. You must take action and plan to do something about it. Examples: A test, losing weight, a sport or talent, spending money, a drug or alcohol problem. Here's some actions:

    TEST - Plan time to study. Talk to friends or the teacher about points where you are having trouble. Check the facts, make a study sheet, study with a friend. STUDY!

    SPENDING MONEY WISELY. Make a budget. (There is one at the end of this chapter.) Make a list of your spending for a week/month. Where are you wasting money? Can you find ways to earn more? Are you an impulsive spender? Carry only a small amount of money with you and *no credit cards.* Ask, "Do I really need this?"

    IMPROVING A SPORT/TALENT - Taking action is making a plan. Make a practice schedule. Talk to a teacher or coach, a parent, relative or a friend. Talk to anyone who is good at this to give you pointers to improve. Take lessons. Read to get some new ideas. Work out with a friend who is good. Practice practice, practice!

    In taking action, remember you have lots of help available. Ask people who have been through it, good at it or who can guide you to help. Go to the library, read books for ideas, take lessons or classes to get better.

21

Whenever there is a problem -a challenge - ask yourself, "Do I accept it, cope, or take action?" If you choose one way to handle your problem and it doesn't work, then choose another way. We learn from our mistakes. Don't be afraid to make mistakes. Think, "What is the worse thing that can happen?" "Can I live through that?" It is better to make a bad or wrong decision than to not make any decision. You can always make another decision. It is a girl's right to change her mind.

TEEN BUDGET

INCOME	EXPENSE
Allowance $_____	**Fixed expenses can't change**
	School lunches $ _____
Babysitting _____	Dues for clubs _____
	Savings account _____
Money gifts _____	Church _____
	Car payment _____
After-school job _____	Car insurance _____
	_____
	_____

Flexible expenses - can change

Snacks	$ _____
School supplies	_____
Clothes	_____
Make-up, nails, hair, etc.	_____
Recreation	_____
Magazines	_____
	_____
	_____

TOTAL INCOME $_____   TOTAL EXPENSES $_____

1. You need to take in more money than you spend. You need to have some money left each month for emergencies. Save this extra money.

2. Keep track of everything you buy for two weeks.

3. Look to see where you spend the most money.

4. Are you wasting your money on anything? What? How can you change it?

5. The fixed expenses CAN NOT be changed. You must pay these. Yours may be different than what is listed here. Make your own list.

6. Flexible expenses CAN be changed. This is where you have control.

7. Don't keep much cash on you. Carry only what you need.

8. Don't get a credit card. This is why even adults go into debt and get in trouble. It is too easy to buy things when you have credit cards.

9. If you must have a credit card, don't carry it. Keep it in a cup of water in the freezer. Then you have time to think about what you want to buy.

10. Do you have a goal for your savings?

Chapter 4

Handling Your Emotions

Annette Fuson

> Jessica is always complaining about everything! She tells everyone else what to do and then complains when things don't go like she expects. "I want to go skating." "That homework Mr. Frank gave wasn't fair." "Jamie is so bossy." She used to be fun, but lately you can't please her. Everyone is tired of her finding fault. Why does she complain so much? How can she change?

Emotions are the basic "ingredient" of girls. In the teen years, emotions are in full bloom because your hormones are raging. This is the time you have to learn control. Emotions are normal, but you can't let them run wild. The following are some common teen emotions. For each one, there are questions for you and help in how you may get control of them.

ANGER - Do you have a temper? Are you angry all the time? What things anger you most? Is it school, parents, brothers or sisters, friends, not getting your way? Is it that you can't do what you want? Are you angry at everything? Really look and keep track of what causes your anger. Why are you angry? What do people do that angers you? Do you destroy things when you're angry? Do you throw things? Do you stay angry?

WHAT TO DO

Keep a chart on your anger: when it happens, what triggers it and how long it lasts. This will help you see a pattern. Do certain people cause you to blow up? It is important to learn to manage your temper. When you are mad, it builds up energy inside of you and you need an acceptable way to channel it. Do something physical: walk, run, play ball, mow the grass, clean your room, scrub a floor, hit a ball. Sometimes talking it out with a friend will help. You must get it out without hurting others. If you break or throw things when you're angry, you have a BIG problem. If you can't control it, talk to your school counselor about anger management classes. You may be holding a lot of resentment inside. A professional can help you.

HURT - Do you wear your feelings on your sleeves? Do you get your feelings hurt easily? Do you feel hurt often? Does it take a lot to hurt you? Do you feel people hurt your feelings on purpose? Do your friends leave you out of things? Does your boyfriend do things to hurt you? Are you sad often? Do you eat too much junk food? Do you get enough sleep? Do people say things to hurt you? Are you sensitive about everything?

WHAT TO DO

It is normal to feel hurt when people do or say things to you that undermine you. If your boyfriend breaks up with you, you'll feel hurt. We don't know why people do these things. Most times

27

they don't do it on purpose. They don't mean to hurt you. When parents or teachers compare us to others, it can hurt. They think it will make us better, but it doesn't. If you feel hurt often, you need to do something for yourself. Mentally, put on a coat of armor to protect yourself from what people say. Go to the library and get a book on self-confidence. Talk to yourself about the good traits you have. Stay away from the people who hurt you. Do things that you enjoy. Have some fun. Be with happy people. Make some new, happy friendships.

JEALOUSY - Do you wish you were someone else? Are you sorry that you aren't as beautiful as a friend? Do you want a big house? Do you wish your parents were rich? Do you envy a friend's figure? Are your grades good? Do you have money to spend? Are you wearing clothes you like? Do you have a talent?

WHAT TO DO

It is **very** common, as a teenage girl, to constantly compare yourself to others and find you aren't as good as you wish. If you had a magic wand to give yourself all you wanted, in a week or two, you'd wish for something else. No matter what you have, it will never satisfy you. That's normal. Some things you're jealous about, you can really achieve with work. Notice what is important to you and what you'd just like. See if you can work toward those important goals. If not, let it go. Enjoy those things about others and know that they are probably wishing they had some things you have. The grass is always greener on the other side of the fence.

SAD/DEPRESSED - Are you sad often? Do you feel depressed only over certain things? Do people depress you? Does not being able to do things sadden you? Are you so sad that you cry a lot? Are you around depressing people? Has this happened lately? Is it only during some times of the month? Do you still function when you're sad? Can you figure out if only certain people cause this? Have you always been an unhappy person? Are you in good health? Do you like being sad? Has something happened in your life to cause this?

WHAT TO DO

Depression and sadness can become a way of life. This in unhealthy. If you are only sad sometimes, that may be normal. If you have figured out that something or someone causes you to feel sad, then you need to deal with that. If you are so depressed that you let your looks go, stay alone, don't want to get out of bed, then you need to see a doctor. There is something serious here. Medication may help you. Diet may also help you and the doctor will suggest what to eat. If this is temporary, you need to be around people who cheer you up. Get into activities that are fun. If this feeling is like pessimism; looking on the bad side of things - then you have a habit to break. People do not like being around people who are gloomy about everything. Why do you do this? You need to work on your self-confidence and self-esteem. When you catch yourself being down and gloomy, turn your thoughts around to something happy or pleasant. If it happens often, think about counseling to help figure out why you are depressed and down. If, however, you are only sad on occasion, that is normal.

COMPLAINING & WHINING - Do you complain constantly? Do you feel nothing goes right? Do you say, "I can't" often? Do you gripe about homework, tests, teachers, friends, and family? Are you unhappy with yourself? Do you whine a lot? Do you enjoy complaining? Do you blame others for your failures? Do you feel others don't like you? Do you find fault with everything? Are people always saying "Quit complaining"? Are you upset often? Are you used to getting your way if you whine? Are you mad about a home problem? Are you taking out your unhappiness on them?

WHAT TO DO

Complaining and whining can easily become a habit. You may not even realize you are doing it. Stop and listen to yourself. Are you complaining only about certain things? That may be legitimate complaining. However, if you find yourself always taking the opposite point of view, then you have a problem. Try to figure out why you are always complaining and whining. Become aware of this habit and do things to stop it. People do not like being around people who always whine and complain. You may be unhappy about your life or something in it. Maybe you don't feel you have any good points or talents. That isn't true, as you learned in the first chapter. Everyone has good points and can do some things well. No one can do everything well. Are you complaining for attention? That is childish! You need to get involved in plays, music, sports or something that you are good at and you'll get "good" attention.

WORRYING - Do you find yourself worrying constantly? Are you always afraid the worst will happen? Do you have headaches or stomach aches? When something bad happens, do you say, "I knew it!" Are you afraid to do things for fear something will happen? Have bad things happened to you often? Is your mother or father a worrier? Do you worry about your looks? About your future? About school or friends? Is there anything that doesn't worry you? Do you have fun in your life? Do you smile or laugh much? Can you see the humor in things? Do people call you a worrywart?

WHAT TO DO

Worrying can be a good trait because it keeps you alert and always thinking. If you are <u>always</u> worrying, that's different and not good, especially if you worry over what might happen. That is spending energy on negative thoughts you could be spending on good and fun things. Worrying all of the time over "what ifs" is silly because it probably won't happen. If it does, then deal with it then. Don't ask for problems and trouble by worrying ahead. You will be able to handle whatever you are worrying about. Or find someone to help you handle the problem. The person who worries constantly loses out on so much fun in life because they are so afraid of what could happen. The person who looks on the bright side of things doesn't worry much. They are happier and more fun to be around. Worrying is a habit. When you start to worry about something, stop and really think, "Am I worrying over nothing?" "Is this really happening?" Then if you need to, change your thoughts. Talk to yourself, "I'll tackle the problem when it comes." This won't be easy, but with work you can change it and you will be a much happier person.

None of these traits are **"What is best for you."**

It is okay to have anxious, scared, angry, depressed or lazy feelings, as long as you don't let them stop you from doing what you have to do. If you find you get really down and moody often, there is medication to help you. It is not normal to be sad and depressed often. Girls often tend to be more emotional than boys are. Girls will be really happy and "up", then get really down. Remember, much of this emotional roller coaster is due to your hormones. Notice which common emotions are "you" and try to do something to overcome them.

Here is a little test to help you be aware of your emotions. Check the statements that apply to you. Then score yourself.

WHICH ARE YOU?

_____ My life often seems to be out of my control.

_____ Much of my life is spent on other people's goals.

_____ I often get into trouble by assuming I know something when I don't.

_____ I have a tendency to expect the worst.

_____ I often find myself saying, "I don't feel up to it."

_____ The fear of appearing stupid often prevents me from asking questions or offering my opinion.

_____ I have trouble taking criticism, even from my friends.

_____ If I'm not perfect, I often feel worthless.

_____ I have trouble focusing on what's really important to me.

_____ I often wish I were someone else.

_____ I find when I really want something, I'll act impulsively to get it.

_____ I often feel irritable and moody.

_____ I waste a lot of time.

_____ I spend time with people who belittle me or put down my thoughts or ideas.

_____ I often do not live up to my potential because I put things off to the last minute.

SCORING

0-2 Your life is very normal.

3-5 You are doing some things that are holding you back. Work a little on self-improvement.

6-11 Remove what's causing you trouble; things will improve.

12-15 You could benefit from some one-on-one help. Talk to a teacher or adult friend for ideas.

Notice the ones you checked. Can you figure out why you have these feelings? Hopefully, you will get ideas and help from this book to change your life's direction. Remember too, there are many people willing to listen and give you guidance. Just always keep in mind the statement: **"Is this what's best for ME?"**

Chapter 5

Building Friendships with Girls

Laticha, 15, is very shy and quiet. She just moved and is starting high school. She walks down the halls and eats lunch alone. She is having trouble making friends. She is so unhappy! She misses her friends from her other school. Laticha enjoys Spanish class and has decided to try out for choir because she loves to sing. She keeps wondering, "Will anyone ever want me as a friend? What can I do to make friends?"

In reality you need lots of friends. You can't have too many. You have friends at school, in sports or activities, at church and in your neighborhood. Then you have that special, best friend. How do you choose friends? Friends are people like you. They have the same interests - (sports, music, reading, hobbies, and band). You may have lots in common: short or tall, quiet, or from the same culture or religion. We tend to like people whose personalities are similar to ours. We understand these people. Usually you have the same values - what you believe is right or wrong. They believe in what you do or don't do. When friends have things in common, they understand each other. They feel comfortable and have many things to talk about. When they like similar things, they have fun together. As you grow older and more confident, you begin to choose other friends with some differences. This is fun, because you learn so much about others who have differences from you.

How to be a friend - There is a saying: "A friend is a present you give yourself." That is so true because you must be friendly in order to make friendships. So when you are friendly, you get the "present" - a new friend! To be friendly, you must smile, say "hi", ask questions about their interests, act interested in them and what happens to them. "How did the test go?" "What happened at practice?" "How was your weekend?" Show caring. Call them. Go places together. Don't expect them to ask you, ask them. Ask them over or to go somewhere. Ask their opinion. Remember their birthday. Do for them what you'd like others to do for you.

What to talk about - The list is endless! Talk about both your interests. Your family, school, classes, teachers, BOYS (of course), books you've read, movies, hair styles, clothes, fads, make-up, articles in magazines, your goals or dreams. Ask their opinions, "what would you do if".... Talk about vacations, hobbies, activities at school. Ask them about themselves. What they like or dislike, their feelings, their experiences. ANYTHING!

Finding friends - You can find friends everywhere. They may move into your neighborhood. A list of activities where they may be are: sports, clubs, scouts, band, choir, lessons or classes in dance, karate, art, ceramics, music, tennis, bowling, ballet, softball, swimming. Volunteer at the hospital, literacy or Big Sister program. Anywhere you go and are involved, look for new girls. Doing these things, you'll have fun, meet others and help people, too.

Traits in friends - There are certain traits that everyone likes in a friend. If you can develop these traits, you'll be a great friend!

1. **BEING KIND AND THOUGHTFUL** - Doing nice things for others. Sending cards when they are sick or on a birthday. Calling them when they are sick or have been away. Congratulating them on accomplishments. Complimenting them on their looks, outfits, things they do well.

2. **BEING RESPONSIBLE** - Being sincere in what you say and do. You are able to tell right from wrong. Thinking and acting responsibly. You are accountable for your actions.

3. **BEING DEPENDABLE** - Being reliable and trustworthy. You will do what you say you will. People can count on your word. This is so important in friendships because when you tell someone you'll go or do something, they want to count on you to do it.

4. **BEING TRUSTWORTHY** - Being able to believe you. You won't lie or cheat. Others can rely on you to stand up for them and not let them down.

5. **BEING HONEST** - Being truthful. You will tell a friend the truth. You are not two-faced and will not talk behind their back. Whatever you say, they know that it is the truth.

6. **BEING FUN** - Willing to try new things. You will give things a chance. You are open-minded to do things

you've never tried if your friend enjoys it. Open to new ideas. Willing to find the humor in things. Laugh and enjoy life.

7. **HAVING A SENSE OF HUMOR** - Seeing the funny side of things. Willing to laugh at yourself. Not being super serious about everything. Being relaxed and able to laugh and find fun in life.

8. **BEING OPTIMISTIC** - Looking on the bright side of things. Able to see the best and make the most favorable point in what will happen. Hold an open view. You believe things in life will turn out for the best.

There are some traits that destroy friendships. Look to see if you have any of these and try to rid yourself of them.

1. **CONCEITED** - Acting stuck-up. You think and act like you are better than everyone else. You have a very high opinion of yourself, to the point of looking down on others.

2. **ARGUMENTATIVE** - Always finding a fight. Wanting to argue or take the opposite side of everything. Not congenial. You like to be controversial.

3. **ALWAYS ANGRY** - Getting mad easily. Wanting to find fault with everyone. Never being happy with things. Wearing a chip on your shoulder, daring others to knock it off.

4. **TWO FACED** - Talking behind others' backs. Saying one thing to people's faces and something different

behind their backs. Saying things that aren't true to others. Acting nice one minute and snotty the next.

5. **STEAL GUYS** - Flirting with guys your friends like. Trying to get other girls' guys. Making a game of going after your friends' boyfriends. Acting innocent about it.

6. **MAKING FUN OF OTHERS** - Belittling others in front of people. Saying nasty names for others to hear. Spreading bad rumors about people to hurt them.

7. **HAVE TO HAVE YOUR WAY** - Thinking your ideas are the only ones. Hogging the spotlight. Not listening to others' opinions. Won't give in.

8. **BEING PESSIMISTIC** - Always looking on the bad side. Thinking everything will turn out wrong. Nothing will go right. Worrying all the time and thinking the worst.

Girl friendships will last a lifetime. You are investing yourself in friendships, so invest wisely. Friends you choose are an extension of yourself. The friends you choose in your teen years will affect you for your whole life. Friends can influence you for good or evil. Make sure you make wise choices. Ask yourself, **"Is this friend what's best for ME?"**

WHAT KIND OF FRIEND ARE YOU?

Put the number in the blank that best tells your feelings.

4 - always   2 - sometimes

3 - most times   1 - seldom

_____ I feel happy

_____ I smile often

_____ I say "hi" to new people

_____ I am willing to try new activities

_____ I take a bath or shower daily

_____ I compliment people

_____ I readily do things my friends want to do

_____ I can take a joke

_____ I refrain from complaining to friends

_____ I enjoy my friends activities

_____ I don't have to have my own way

_____ I try not to argue with friends

_____ I am a responsible person

_____ I have values of my own

_____ I usually like people

_____ I'm friendly

_____ I look on the bright side of things

_____ I feel good with the people around me

_____ I am tolerant of others feelings

_____ I try not to find fault with others

_____ I enter into sports, music or hobbies

_____ I like myself

_____ I offer to help others

_____ I am considerate of others feelings

_____ I am glad when good things happen to others

_____ I am an up-beat person

_____ I like to do fun things

_____ I turn down drugs and alcohol

_____ I feel I'm a good listener

_____ I am honest and truthful

_____ I do what I say I will

_____ I am willing to share

_____ I am trustworthy

_____ I am kind to others

_____ I take care of my looks

_____ I am willing to do what my friend wants

_____ I share my feelings and thoughts

_____ My friends can count on me

_____ I do nice things for my friends

_____ I invite my friends to do things with me

Add them up:

Above 140   Exceptional friend. People enjoy you.

125-139   Excellent friend. People want your friendship.

115-124   Good qualities, but work on more "most times"(3) or "always" (2).

100-114   Fair. You need to think of others' more than self.

42

80-99   You need to work on friendship qualities. Read the chapter again. Think where you need help. You have to BE a friend to have a friend.

Some of the most important qualities are numbers 2, 6, 9, 20, 24, 31, 34, and 38. Concentrate on these and friends will come.

Chapter 6

Boys vs. Girls

Michelle and Jason, both 14, have been friends for years. They are neighbors, playing together and sharing secrets since third grade. They have always enjoyed each other's company, but lately Jason has changed. He has been acting silly, teasing Michelle and doing dumb things for attention. She can't figure out what's wrong with him. She has been thinking maybe it's her because she's been moody and gets upset easily. She keeps wondering, "What could it be? What can I do? Why has he changed?"

...Boys, boys, boys! You will suddenly be at an age when that is ALL you'll be able to think about. When you're a young teen, you think boys are stupid and silly. You don't want to have anything to do with them. Then as you get older, one special boy will turn you to butter! HE is all you'll think about, talk about and dream about. Your friends will get so tired of hearing about him. Then you won't like him anymore and another boy will come into your life. Boys will fill your life with laughter...and tears. You will love them...and hate them. Your feelings about boys will be exhilarating as well as depressing. Learning some things about them will help you understand them.

Boys don't mature as soon as girls. Therefore, they will seem immature to you. They do dumb things, such as fight and push each other to show off. They talk, brag and tease trying to make girls think they are big stuff. However, usually they are not so sure of themselves. As they get older and more experienced, they feel more secure, but girls will always be a mystery to them. This is because boys and girls are so different.

Mother Nature plays a cruel joke in making boys slower to mature. They are shorter than girls for a couple years. This is very embarrassing for them. Then their voice begins to change. Sometimes it is low and sometimes high, but they never know how it will come out. Can you blame them for being quiet? They don't like being made fun of any more than you do. When their bodies begin to change, they seem to grow in pieces. Their arms and legs or hands and feet grow first. That makes them clumsy and gangly looking. They are awkward with the new long arms and legs. It is a while before their body catches up. This is very embarrassing to them, because they can't help it.

Boys are interested in things that are powerful. They enjoy such things as cars, motors, computers, gadgets, sports and video games. They like to do things to prove to themselves that they have power and control. It is important to boys to have control over things they do. They want to do well. When boys know what they are doing, and are in control, it makes them feel more secure and masculine. They feel dumb and insecure when they don't know how things will turn out. That's why they won't dance or enter into activities that are new. They need advance notice so they can figure out what to do. Power includes speed. You'll notice boys are always moving. They run, jump, hit, kick and push; especially when a couple of guys get together. They love challenges. Therefore things like sports and video games fascinate them. If they are in a sport, it is the number one thing in their life. Girls are always second. You have to accept that. Then when they are old enough to drive, their car is first in their life. It is all they talk about...car, car, car.

They like girls, but at first they are afraid of them. They don't understand girls. Girls talk too much, they giggle a lot and they act like they don't care about boys. If they only knew. It takes being around girls as friends and in groups for a year or two before boys realize that girls are okay.

Boys generally are more quiet than girls are. They don't want to chance making a fool of themselves by saying something dumb and being laughed at. They tend to keep problems inside and don't ask for help. They try to figure things out on their own, so they like being alone. Boys seem to hide their true thoughts. When they do things, they are more exact, not as general. They like things to happen in a certain order and to be done a certain way. They concentrate on one thing at a time. They will accomplish one thing before they go to another. This way it can be done right and they have more control over it. When they have to do several things at once, they become frustrated. Understanding how they feel will help you in dealing with them.

Boys worry about things the same as you do: that people will make fun of them, that they won't fit in to a group, that they won't be good at things they do, that friends will leave them, that they'll never get a girl, that they'll get too fat or their face will break out. These are normal fears for all teens and you have to do the best you can and develop a sense of humor to handle it all. Just remember, the short, pimple-faced, awkward, shrill voice, quiet boy may become the "handsome prince," so you had better be nice to them all.

Girl's Differences - Girls are very different from boys in how they behave and look at things. You are more emotional, more talkative and more interested in people's opinions. You are always sharing your opinions, how you do things, how you feel, your clothes and your problems. You LOVE talking on the phone and being with friends. You care what other people think, and love giving advice. You like to do several things at once, not just one. You can be babysitting, talking on the phone, doing your nails and watching TV all at once. It doesn't seem to matter to you if you are doing each job perfectly. Girls are impulsive. You do things first and think later, not concerned about the outcome. Being in control is not as important to you.

Girls' worries are endless. You worry about your looks, if people will like you, if friends will drop you and if you'll do something stupid. You worry about what other people will think of you and if that isn't enough, your body is beginning to change - another worry. Some of you will mature sooner, some later. Some will get a big bustline, others a small one. Your body is going to change and you have no control over that. You will learn to handle it. (You don't want to look like a 10-year-old forever.) Your emotions will run rampant. Some things will come out of your mouth and you'll wonder who said them. You'll be high and happy one minute, then crying and down the next. You'll wonder what is happening to you and so will all those around you. Talk over your fears and questions with your mother, sister, aunt, teacher or any adult you trust. Knowing what to expect will help you make it through these times more successfully.

The changes in your body and your moods are caused by hormones. Hormones go throughout the body and start the maturing process. You get taller, your figure starts to develop, your menstrual period begins, your face may break out, your hair gets oily and your emotions are on a roller coaster. Just take it one day at a time. This is all natural. Everyone goes through these things. If you are involved in school, church or other activities, it will pass smoothly and quickly. Don't be afraid to try new things. Every new experience you have will make you a better person. You aren't thinking of yourself so much when you are involved. Go out and experience new things. You make the choices because **you are in charge of your life!**

Boy/Girl Friendships - Building boy-girl friendships is much like building girl friendships. You smile, say "Hi," and act friendly. In talking to boys, ask about interests they have: school, activities, sports, favorite classes or teachers, music, movies, books, friends, family and their car. Treat them like yourself. Play some fun games like card games, dominoes, trivia, Scrabble, Monopoly and other board games. Participate in sports: tennis, badminton, bowling, croquet, swimming, volleyball, catch or skating with boys. Do things like crafts or a hobby, cook or bake, paint a room or furniture. Volunteer to help people: rake leaves, mow, shovel snow, wash windows or run errands. Do a community project. Your school and church have a variety of activities, too. When you do things together like these, you talk and have fun, but you learn about each other, also. This helps you both to become more well rounded individuals. When your heart flips over a special boy, these ideas will work for him, too. Kissing and touching are fun too, but you need to have lots of other things to do. Life with boys will have its ups and downs. As you mature and grow into a happy adult, the main thing is to enjoy life.

Chapter 7

Getting Out of Bad Situations

Candice, 16, is allowed to go with boys. She has been seeing Eric, 17. She is excited, but also afraid. She has seen a lot of TV stories where girls get into terrible situations and scary things happen to them. She has known Eric for a long time and feels she can trust him, but some of his new friends act weird. Candice wants to go out and have fun, but she's not secure in knowing if she can handle things on her own. She knows she needs help. "What do I do if Eric wants to go places that I can't? What if his friends influence him? How can I feel more confident with my decisions?"

Everyone finds themselves in situations where they don't want to be. Being a teenager, you can often find yourself in bad situations. Teens need ideas on how to avoid these situations.

Know your values - The first thing you need to do is take a hard look at your own values. What do you believe is right and wrong? Knowing what you personally think and how far you believe you want to go in **each** situation will help you when it happens. So, as you mature and your experiences change, **before** you get into the situation, THINK, what do you want to happen?

Situations - There are several kinds of situations that are dangerous for you.

1. When you are over your head and everyone else is more experienced.

2. When there are older kids involved.

3. When the boy you are with is older and more experienced.

4. When everyone else seems to have different values than you.

5. When the place you are going is off limits - his apartment, no adults around, very secluded, a fraternity house.

6. When others are getting high or drunk.

7. When the people are wild and out of control.

8. When you feel forced to do or try things that you don't want to do.

9. When you feel yourself lying or stealing to impress friends.

10. When you are asked to leave a game or party early. That leaves too much time available to get into trouble before you have to be home.

This means that you need to think ahead. "Am I going to be put in a situation I can't or don't want to handle?" It is much easier to use an excuse to <u>not</u> get in the situation than it is to try to have to get out of it. You can say, "I can't go, my Mom won't let me." "My parents would kill me!" "I have to get up early tomorrow and go to my aunt's house." "The coach makes us get in early." Don't get in a bad situation, then you don't have to get out of one.

Kind of Friends - What kind of friends do you have? Are their beliefs like yours? Do they like to do what you like? Do they make you feel guilty? Do they call you a baby or ask if you are afraid to try things? Do they have their interests in mind, or yours? Sometimes the friends you choose are your problem. You may need to choose other friends. You may be surprised at who puts you on the spot. You could say, "Smoking makes me sick." "I'm allergic to alcohol." "No, I don't want to try that." "My dad would kill me!" "It's not my thing." "I don't feel good tonight." Then make sure you don't go out with them again. Friends may want you to smoke, drink alcohol or take drugs.

As you know, smoking makes your breath and clothes smell, and your teeth turn yellow. It forms lines around your mouth and you can develop lung cancer. These are facts we know. Besides, it is expensive. Save that money for clothes and jewelry. Smoking does <u>not</u> make you look cool.

Drinking and using drugs is a whole new story. They really ruin your health and life. The biggest problem for you is you lose your sense of what's right or wrong when you are high or drunk. You won't even remember what you did. Now that's really dangerous. People can take advantage of you. In fact, some people will make you drunk or high so they can take advantage of your body. Ann Landers says: "A good rule to remember is: when the booze or drugs goes in, the resistance goes down. Alcohol or drugs and youthful hormones can be a dangerous combination!"

Alcohol and drugs are not only bad for your health and body; they are bad for your future and goals. Remember, **"Is this what's best for me!"**

Sex - It is a fact; if you are alone with a boy for very long kissing and touching, **IT WILL GO TOO FAR**! One of the biggest differences between boys and girls is how they react sexually. This is important. Boys get sexually excited QUICKLY - like, in 2 to 3 minutes! They get "hot" from things they see and think: a girl's body in tight clothes, no bra, low neck, short skirt, or what they think might happen. They may become SO excited that they can't think straight. They just want to do whatever they can to "score."

Girls are much slower to get excited. Therefore, you can keep your head longer. That means you need to be in charge of the situation. You need to cool things off. You need to be aware that if you dress in a sexy, suggestive way - clothes too short, too tight, and too low - it will get the boy's hormones roaring. He may try things, thinking you want him to. Then if you stop him and act hurt, he calls you a "tease." Boys don't like that. YOU control the situation. You are also the one that can get pregnant if it goes too far.

The boy may use his lines on you. He says something to make you go ahead to "home base." These lines are used to make you feel guilty:

1. "What's wrong, are you afraid?"
2. "Are you chicken or a baby?"
3. "Don't you trust me?"
4. "I thought you loved me."
5. "If you love me, show it."
6. "Surely you are old enough to make up your own mind."

Other lines try to wear you down:

1. "Everybody does it."
2. "I won't let anything happen to you."
3. "I won't tell anyone."
4. "People will think we did it anyway."
5. "Why wait?"
6. "Take a chance, live a little."
7. "It will clear up your face."

The **BIG** line is when he says "Love." To girls, it is important that he loves you. Remember, it is easy to **say!** If he truly loved you, he'd want what is best for you, not him.

8. "I love you, I'll protect you."
9. "If you loved me, you'd make me happy."
10. "Show me that you love me."
11. "People who love each other do it."
12. "If you don't, I'll find someone who will."

You should practice some answers:

1. "If you loved ME, you'd wait until I'm ready."
2. "I'm not ready yet."
3. "I'm not like everybody else."
4. "Why would you put me on the spot?"

Things to do - The best and easiest thing for you to do is something BEFORE it gets to the "skin on skin" point. Do something to change the atmosphere. You can do one or two of the following so he can have time to cool off and get his head back.

1. Hold his hand, tightly.
2. Stiffen your body or wiggle around.
3. Move his hand away from your breast.
4. Say you "heard a noise."
5. "My folks will be back soon."
6. Get a cramp in your foot or leg.
7. Pretend your foot is asleep and bounce it.
8. Say you have a headache.
9. Fake a pain in your side.
10. Pretend he tickled you.
11. Laugh - because you thought of something funny.
12. Tickle him
13. …Or anything else you can think of.

Then say:…

1. "It's late, I have to go."
2. "We're getting too carried away."
3. "I'm not ready for this."
4. "I don't want either of us to feel bad tomorrow for what we did tonight."

You must be ready for bad situations because they will happen to you. No one will be there to help you, so you need to think ahead and be ready. Practice what you will say and do. Be prepared with your answers. **<u>Say them with firmness</u>**! Don't be wishy-washy. Don't say, "I don't **think** I should." Be firm. Don't let other people make choices for you. They may not have your best interest in mind, but **their** best interest. Others may give you ideas and examples to help you make a decision, but **you** make the final choice.

To review:
1. Know your own values.
2. Realize ahead how far you want to go.
3. Choose your friends carefully.
4. Don't get "IN" the situation and you won't have to get "OUT" of it.

5. Practice what you'll say and do.

6. Know what is best for you.

7. What are your goals for your future?

8. ALWAYS ask**, "Is this what's best for ME?"**

Chapter 8

Understanding Sex

> Tara, 17, and her boyfriend Jared, 18, have been dating for two or three months. At first they were always with lots of their friends, but lately he only wants to be with her. He takes her somewhere secluded. When alone, his kisses get long and passionate and his hands wander all over her body. They both become very excited. Last time Jared started to unzip her jeans, but she held his hand hard to stop him. Tara feels very confused and is not sure what she wants to happen next. She asks herself, "What do I do? How do I know if I'm ready for this?"

Sex is everywhere. Sex sells magazines. It is in advertisements, in the movies and on television. There is nothing left to the imagination anymore. On shows, people get into bed with people they don't even know. It leads you to believe that everyone does it and it is the answer to all of your problems. WRONG! Everyone does not do it, and it can make more problems than you can imagine. TV shows and movies have so many sexual scenes that it clouds your mind into believing that this is normal behavior. You feel out of it when you choose not to do it. There is pressure from your peers and your boyfriend. It is very hard to sort out your feelings when there is so much pressure everywhere.

Remember, boys have very little to lose if they go too far sexually. They don't get a bad reputation and they can't get pregnant. They also get pressured by other boys to score with girls. They sometimes make sex a sport and belittle the guy that doesn't go along. They talk about girls and what they've done with them. This doesn't sound very nice, but it is a fact you should know.

If you are a young teen, just enjoy boys as friends. Go in groups, stay focused and do fun things. There are lots of ideas in the chapter 6, "Boys vs. Girls", that will help you learn about boys and how they think, how they are different and what you like and dislike about them. It will protect you from having to make a decision about sex. This will give you time to mature. You will have more faith in yourself before you have to make the "big" decision.

If you are an older teen, you may find yourself liking a boy a lot. It is a situation where you have to make some hard decisions. Now you are in a position where you need to do some thinking BEFORE you make "the decision".

Sexual intercourse will change your relationship with your boyfriend. That may become all he wants to do. The focus will become "when can we be alone and do it". Your view of yourself will change. You may feel used, betrayed, guilty and like your feelings won't be important any more. It becomes such a BIG decision because you can't take it back.

Sex is meant to be a wonderful experience, *not* entertainment or a contact sport. Sex is supposed to be an expression of love with both people wanting to give their feelings of love to the other. Each person wanting to bring happiness to the other. It is not self satisfying, but giving. Teens usually don't have these feelings because it takes maturity to think of the other person ahead of yourself.

Meaningful sexual experiences happen when you are older, more mature, wiser and more responsible. You think before you act. You realize that the guy truly loves you because he is committed or you are married. Therefore you feel safe and secure. Sex is suppose to be an experience of warmth and happiness, as well as, exhilarating, and thrilling. But it should always **feel right**.

As a teen, it is usually a bad experience. Teenage girls' minds are unclear. You are led into sex and most times you regret the decision to have sex. Because you are young or inexperienced, sex becomes forced or rushed. Afterwards you regret what you've done. This can be so disappointing. Once you have sex, you are no longer a virgin and you can never get that back. That may be a big deal to you or it may not. Either way, the decision should be made with maturity. It is better to look forward to something and not regret it, than to regret it and have nothing to look forward to.

Go slowly. There are lots of things you can do to show that you care for each other besides sexual intercourse. There is a normal sequence. Holding hands, hugging, teasing and kissing. You can do a lot of kissing, hugging and touching that will satisfy both of you without getting you into trouble. In the last chapter you learned important things to help you keep control.

1. Boys get excited faster and can't think
2. You control it because you are excited slower
3. Boys may use lines to break you down.
4. You have answers you can use (see chapter7).
5. You must control the situation
6. Don't get in the situation and you won't have to get out of it.
7. Say "I care about you and I don't want either of us to feel bad tomorrow because of something we did tonight".

You may ask yourself, "What is too far?" You decide, of course, but kissing and hugging is okay. Even deep kissing and some touching - outside of clothes. You can do these things for months without going farther. What gets dangerous is "third base" - clothes get pulled over, unzipped or taken off. Skin touching skin gets the hormones going. You may as well light a match to dynamite because you are starting to blast off. At least he will be! His breathing will be fast, or he may become aggressive and demanding with no thought of you. NOW you are close to sex.

There are so many dangers for you as a teen. There are all kinds of sexually transmitted diseases (STD) - herpes, syphilis and gonorrhea - to name a few. Then there is AIDS. No one ever dreamed that having sex could kill you. Then came AIDS. That is a terrible price to pay for 10 -15 minutes of sex. You can't tell who has these diseases and who doesn't. They can be clean or dirty, rich or poor, smart or dumb - anyone.

These are terrible things to have happen to you, but there is another worry: the possibility of getting pregnant. For a teen to bring another person into the world when you yourself are not mature is so unfair to the baby. Some teens get pregnant on purpose because they want something to love and they think the baby will love them and be fun. They forget a baby is not a toy or doll you can put away when you don't want to mess with it. A baby is a tremendous responsibility and a great deal of work. It cries, sometimes a lot, all day and night. It messes its pants; it spits up and smells bad. It needs CONSTANT attention. It will become a two-year-old and a teenager. You have to deal with all ages, not just a baby. Your teen years are times for fun, friends, freedom and maturity. Some teens think their mother or grandmother will raise the baby. That is truly not responsible. A teen is very selfish when she thinks someone will raise her child. A baby is a responsibility for 18 years. The baby needs lots of love, patience, guidance, work, care and money. Teens are not ready for all that. So you must think ahead.

YOU CHOOSE YOUR BEHAVIOR. If you feel you're ready for sex, then you should be responsible enough to practice safe sex so you won't have any of these problems. Planned Parenthood or your family doctor will help you make safe choices as to what birth control is available, if you have no one else to help you.

There is something else that happens to some girls when they have sex. Something that can't be seen. That is shame and remorse. This happens when you go against your beliefs; you do something that you believe is wrong. The mind is funny, it continues to think when you don't want it to. The mind knows your beliefs, regrets, worries and it keeps thinking, making you feel guilty and upset. It doesn't stop. So you want to think this through *before* you act.

You may be asking, "How will I know when I'm ready for sex?" If a voice inside of you says, "NO, stop! This isn't what I want to do," then you are NOT ready yet. When you are ready, you will know because you won't hear a voice. It will seem right. You, hopefully, will be older, wiser and sure of yourself. You will not have any doubts.

Another thing, boys think of sex differently than girls. Sex means two things to them. Especially when they are young, sex is an act. It is something to do, a release for them. Later when they fall in love, then sex is an act of love. Boys separate the two, while girls associate sex with love. They generally don't have sex unless they "love" the boy and they think he loves them. This is hard to understand.

Boys can have sex with lots of girls and they seldom get a bad reputation. They are just getting experience. If a girl has sex with several guys, then people talk about her and she gets a bad reputation and is called a slut. Nice guys won't go with her and other guys just use her for their sexual pleasure. She's called promiscuous.

It is not fair, but being a girl, you must control the sexual situation because you have so much more to lose when it gets out of hand. You can handle it. Give some thought about where you want your life to go…your goals and dreams. Don't let anything or anyone let you change it. Make your right choices. Always think: **"Is this what's best for ME?"**

Chapter 9

Mistakes…
Never too Late!

> Madison, 16, is angry with her parents. They have the same argument over and over. They don't want her to hang out with her college age friends. She realizes the last time she was with them she took some pills to get "spun-out", but she thinks she can handle it. They had some "coke", but she didn't try it. Madison thinks her parents don't trust her. These friends make her feel important. She thinks she can handle it. She's confused, "why are my parents so against these friends?"

Mistakes are normal. Everyone makes mistakes. Mistakes don't have to pull you down. You can learn from your mistakes. It is never too late to fix a mistake. Mistakes come from making bad choices or wrong decisions. They come from being with the wrong person or being easily led by them. Mistakes come from not thinking ahead or mostly not thinking... **"Is this what best for ME?"** You have NO control over other people; you only have control over yourself! Your mistakes will affect others. You've learned in chapter 7, "Getting Out of Bad Situations", that you have to learn to cope or take action when it comes to other people. Other people can't use you without your permission. In other words, you must lie down to be stepped on! So you've made a big mistake. Now let's learn from it and go on from there. It is

NEVER too late to change. You just have to want to change. Let's look at some of the mistakes that girls make and see what might be done now.

CHOOSING FRIENDS - Mistakes come from being with the wrong crowd or wrong friends. Usually, you choose friends that have things in common with you. However, in your teen years, you change as you mature. Your early friends may not feel like you do now. You don't share the same values anymore. They don't like to do the things you enjoy. You can outgrow each other. So what can you do to get away from this crowd or these friends?

1. Gradually arrange to "be busy" when they want to go places or do things.
2. Get involved in school, church or other social activities.
3. Join a gymnastic class, dance group, etc... whatever your interests are.
4. Take lessons such as: ice skating, photography, music, crafts, karate, sports, etc.
5. Get involved in community activities: Young Democrats or Republicans, Big Sister program, Scouts, drama.
6. Take a community education class at a junior college.
7. Get an after-school or Saturday job.
8. Do volunteer work such as helping a teacher after school or at the hospital, join a literacy program to teach reading.

You may have other ideas that will enable you to get away from your questionable friends and make new friends. "If it is to be it is up to me!" That must be your new motto.

> Dalanya is 15 and everyone is talking about her. They aren't saying good things. The girls don't want to be seen with her, but she is the center of the conversation with the guys. They all want a chance to be with her. Dalanya can't see what's wrong with letting guys do things they want to do so they'll be happy. They enjoy her doing things to them too. "Why are the girls shunning me? Why won't the guys take me out? What's wrong with what I'm doing."

BEING PROMISCUOUS - Have you made the mistake of letting boys use your body however they want, and now people call you names? Boys pass your name around to other boys, but no one takes you to a game, movie or party. If this has happened to you and now you regret it, life is NOT over! You have already taken the first step. You have decided you don't want to do it anymore and want to stop. This won't be easy, but lots of girls have done it and you can too. The best answer is to move away and start over, but that is usually not possible. So what do you do? First, it is your word against the boys'. When a new guy approaches you, say, "No, I don't do that," or "You've got me all wrong." If he persists, then just say, "Not anymore!" If you go out with a boy and you think he's nice, then he tries something, again be determined and say "NO!" SLOWLY the word will get around that you've changed. You need to make new friends now. Some girls will be skeptical and it will take time, but it will be worth it. Get involved in things to keep you busy; get a job, volunteer, take lessons, etc. You'll meet new people. Take a class on dressing, wardrobe and make-up. Change your looks. Talk to a trusted teacher for confidence. If you can, stay away from those talkative boys. Just go one day at a time with your new goal and you will make it. Deciding to stop this behavior takes a lot of courage, but you can do it!

> At 17, Tiffany was in deeper than she thought. It all started innocently enough with just a couple beers when friends were together. She had been 15 years old when her boyfriend Austin, 18, insisted she drink to relax. Pretty soon it was a regular thing to see how much you could drink to pass out. The next thing she knew Austin dared her to take a hit with him. That was a year ago; now it was a regular occurrence. Her grades have fallen, she cuts classes, she's always arguing with her mom and nothing seems fun anymore. She asks herself, "What has happened to me? What do I do now?"

DRUGS AND ALCOHOL- With all the pressures around you, it is so easy to make the mistake of getting involved with drugs or alcohol. Alcohol is glorified in the movies and on TV. It may be easy to attain. Teens see parents drink, so teens think it makes you grown-up. (It doesn't) Kids will start with beer and think you can't get hooked with it. A few beers are only the beginning. Sadly, some parents think teenage drinking is not all that bad. If you are to the place that you think you can't have a good time without drinking, then you are hooked!

Alcohol increases the likelihood that you could get sexually assaulted. It increases your vulnerability. Someone can easily take advantage of you. Be aware of how much you have had to drink so you can continue to think clearly. Boys often become more aggressive when they drink. They will not take "no" for an answer They may ignore you or convince themselves that "no" means "yes". The boy's judgement becomes impaired and he may get more forceful. If you are drinking, you may not see the danger. You will not be thinking clearly enough to set limits, resist or communicate clearly.

1. Know your limits in drinking
2. Don't drive and drink
3. Don't ride with someone who has been drinking
4. Don't be alone with someone who is drinking
5. Know what you are drinking
6. Practice what you would do or say if you are in a bad situation

Many teens go from alcohol to drugs, while some girls get involved with drugs first. Generally, an older friend will introduce you to something to "make you relax," "have a good time" or "get high." They can be VERY persuasive and talk you into it. If you are drunk or high, then boys can do whatever they want with your body, and you may not even remember what happened. There are many dangerous drugs. Some drugs are making it easy to victimize you. Rohypnol (Roofies, Rope) and GHB (Camma-Oh, Easy Lay) are two that are cheap and easy to get. They are usually put in a drink without your knowledge. It works in minutes and you won't know what is happening or remember anything. These drugs can cause seizures, respiratory arrest or death! Another dangerous drug is Ecstasy. Those who use this drug for very long find they can't remember things. They act like they have Alzheimer's, which is an old person's disease. Scientists are finding "holes" in the brain of Ecstasy users. That's scary. You need to be aware.

1. Don't drink anything YOU didn't open
2. Don't share drinks
3. Don't leave your drink unattended
4. Don't take a drink offered you
5. Don't drink anything that looks or tastes funny
6. Choose someone in the group to stay sober to watch things and drive

There are MANY other harmful drugs and people waiting for you to get hooked. Educate yourself. Don't be taken in by free samples to make you feel good. Don't start. It is YOUR life. Take control of it.

The real problem with drugs or alcohol is that they are addictive. You think you can stop and you can't. They are also expensive and can ruin your health, as well as bring unhappiness to your family.

So if this was your mistake and you want to stop, what can you do? It will not be easy. It will take a long time and lots of work and commitment. But you can do it. If you've decided to stop, you've taken the first step. You will need help. This is not something you can handle alone.

1. Stay away from people who drink or use drugs.
2. Talk to a school counselor, minister, mother or adult friend for support.
3. Change friends. You can't quit if they don't.
4. Look in the telephone book for:
   > Drug and alcohol abuse
   >
   > Alcoholics' Anonymous (AA)
   >
   > Alateen
   >
   > National Council on Alcohol and Drugs
   >
   > Crisis Intervention

   (These people have teen counselors to help you.)
5. Check the internet:
   > www.health.org
   >
   > www.ncadd.org
   >
   > www.al-anon.org
   >
   > www.ncpc.org/teens/drugalc.html
   >
   > www.ncpc.org/dontlose.html

Call 1-800-622-2255
1-800-729-6686
1-800-SAY-NOTO
1-800-662-HELP

If the person you choose to talk to doesn't respond, then talk to another person. The drug and alcohol organizations deal with your problem every day, so they will be able to evaluate you and decide what would help you best. You may need rehabilitation. You will also need to find new friends and STAY AWAY from your old ones. (This is important!) Take one day at a time. Stay in touch with your counselor. If you slip, that is not the end. Get up and go again. Thousands of other girls have made it and you can too!! Good luck.

> Dawn was 15 when she became pregnant. She didn't expect that this would ever happen to her. Her boyfriend, Brian, 17, had assured her she wouldn't get pregnant. Now he has left her to face it alone. She's afraid to tell her mother for fear of what she'll do. Dawn realizes now that she should have handled things differently. "Why didn't I control the situation? What can I do now?"

GETTING PREGNANT - If you are pregnant, you have three choices. None of them are "good" choices and each will affect your life forever in different ways. You can get an abortion, give the baby up for adoption or keep the baby. To make this decision, it would be best to talk to professionals who can give you information to make the best decision for you and the child. Think it through thoroughly and make sure it is YOUR decision.

If you choose abortion or adoption, then you can go on with your life and plans. However, if you are going to continue to be sexually active, then use birth control so you won't have this choice again. Remember though, birth control does NOT protect you from STD or AIDS, only pregnancy.

Here we will discuss keeping your baby to raise and trying to continue your life. It is important for you and your child to see that you make goals and do something with your life.

1. Finish high school - this is very important for your self worth. Some schools have programs to bring the baby to school. You could find a sitter or go to night school or correspondence school.

2. Plan a career - go to college or training school. You need to get some training or schooling so you can have a decent job to support your baby. Yes, you'll need to find sitters. But this will be short term. Trade sitting with someone else.

3. There are groups that can help - Department of Human Services, church groups, family help groups. All these will help with food, milk, lodging and things for the baby.

4. Planned Parenthood - will give you information and guidance with birth control and sexual questions.

The main thing is to show motivation and determination to get through this and better yourself, as well as the situation. Don't rely on your mother or grandmother to take over for your mistake. You will feel SO much better about yourself when you follow your plan. Now do it!

It was her stepfather that she hated! Tasha, 14, couldn't stand the sight of him. He had been sneaking into her room now for two years, whenever her mother was at work. She was depressed and crying all the time. She couldn't keep her mind on her schoolwork. She had quit the soccer team because she couldn't stand undressing in the locker room. Tasha felt sick to her stomach just thinking about his hands on her one more time! He had told her over and over, "If you tell anyone, I'll hurt you <u>and</u> your mother!" She had to do something. "Why did this happen to ME?", she wondered. Her friends were starting to ask questions and wanted to know what was wrong because she was sad so often. "What can I do? Who can help me?"

MOLESTATION- Being molested is not your mistake, but you are involved and need guidance to get out of the situation. A relative or friend is abusing and molesting you. It may have been happening for several years and now you realize you want it to stop! This was **NOT YOUR FAULT!** It is the molester's problem! They are older and have been using fear as power over you to keep you silent. Sadly, they may be your father, uncle or grandfather. Someone very close and dear to you. It doesn't matter. It should never happen. These people take advantage of your youth and innocence to make you do what they want. Because they may be someone close to you, it makes it very hard to do something to stop it. But you must! It is for your own sake and sanity. What to do:

1. Call Child Abuse Hotline 1-800-252-5400.

   They will guide you to help in your area.

2. Look in the telephone book for:

   Child protective Services

   Child Advocacy Center

   Crisis Center

These groups will guide you on what to do. They even have counseling to help you.

3. Get on the Internet.

   www.rainn.org

   www.apa.org/pi/pii/teen/homepage.html

   www.empowered.org

   www.loveisnotabuse.com

4. Call 1-800-799-SAFE or 1-800-656-HOPE or 1-800-TRY-NOVA

5. Also call 1-800-399-0990 or 1-800-252-5400 or 1-800-537-2238.

6. Call the police - what this person is doing is against the law.

7. There may be a teen shelter in your town to protect you.

8. Buy a bolt lock and install it on your bedroom door. Do it when no one is home and when they ask, say, "I need privacy and want to feel safe."

9. Tell a trusted adult that is NOT a relative. Sorry, but sometimes mother and relatives don't want to believe what's happening and won't do anything.

10. Now DO IT for your own sake. NOW!

Amanda, 18, couldn't understand what had changed. Manuel, 20, and she had been going together for six months. At first things were great! He was so proud of her being on the team. He told her how to improve her looks. He gave her advice on her friends and activities. Lately, though, Manuel gets angry when she wants to do things her way. He was furious when she went to Marie's without telling him. Amanda feels smothered. She can't make a decision without his approval. Yet he tells her he loves her and wants what is best for her. She doesn't know where to turn for help. "Why is this happening to me? How can I change him?"

CONTROLLING AND ABUSIVE BOYFRIENDS - Having a boyfriend should be fun! You should enjoy being with him and not be afraid. You both should share common interests, goals and needs. When you care about someone, you have their best interests in mind, not your own. Are you in a relationship where you feel safe and at peace? Are you free to make your own choices of friends, what to wear, where to go and what to do? Do you feel free to be who **you** want to be? If you answered "no" to any of these questions, then go to "Test Your Boyfriend" (at the end of this chapter) and find out if your boyfriend is the right one for you.

Some boys have a problem with relationships. They must be in control of the other person. This "control" may be making sure you do EVERYTHING he wants. It may be that he controls your mind, so that you think like he wants. In some cases, he uses force to get you to do what he wants...like hitting or slapping. When any of these happen to you, you lose your freedom to be who YOU want to be. Free people can choose what they want and feel good about it. They are not forced to do things to please others. In a good relationship, both people allow the other person to make choices for themselves. They feel safe and secure in the relationship, not afraid. They want what is best for each other, not what is best for them! You should feel free to communicate your feelings to each other. Real love cares how the other feels. If he really loved you, he wouldn't want to hurt you. Abuse it NOT love!

A destructive person wants to tear you apart and then blame you for what happens. This is NOT love. He will act hurt and make you feel guilty. He will lie and be deceptive. Trust is the most important ingredient in a relationship. When people are honest with each other the relationship gets stronger. You feel at peace. You feel safe and you never have to worry. Jealousy is not a sign of love. It is a sign of insecurity. Don't be fooled.

You have a right to your opinion. Opinions aren't right or wrong, only our beliefs. You "own" your feelings and should not be told by him what to believe. You have no control over how someone else feels. He *chooses* to be angry! You should not tolerate harmful behavior. You are not someone else's property to be owned. Don't get involved with someone who's not good for you.

Look at yourself. Are you always drawn to boys who are not good for you? Do you feel you are not worthy of being treated well? Do you get into relationships with self-centered, controlling guys? Maybe you need to find out why. You need to talk to someone trained in helping you. At the end of this chapter there are helpful ideas for you. NO ONE should be a punching bag for someone else! Why are you taking it? You need to decide what you'll put up with in a dating situation. This is your life! Are you living it like **you** want?

If you answered "yes" to ten or more of the questions for "Test Your Boyfriend" (at the end of this chapter), then your boyfriend has control over you. He is **not** going to change. You can not change him. Anyone can apologize and say they'll change. IT WON'T HAPPEN!

Ask yourself:

1. Why am I taking it?
2. Why do I let him treat me badly?
3. Why, to please him, am I being someone I'm not?
4. Why do I settle for less than I deserve?
5. Why am I losing myself by pretending I'm someone I'm not?
6. Why am I letting him get away with it?
7. Why don't I get help and get away?

THIS IS <u>NOT</u> YOUR FAULT!
THINGS YOU COULD SAY TO HIM:

1. Be honest and tell him how you feel. (There are not right or wrong feelings.)

    a) "I don't like it when you are critical and say mean things to me."

    b) "You say you care, but you don't act like it."

    c) "Don't call me names, I don't like it."

    d) "It hurts my feelings when you call me that."

    e) "If you love me, why do you hurt me?"

2. Allow space and time for both of you to think things out.

    a) "I won't allow things to continue as they have been."

    b) "I don't want to see you anymore when you treat me like this."

    c) "I don't deserve this kind of treatment."

    d) "I don't want to see you for awhile. This is a big problem for me."

3. Say what you think.

    a) "I am going to go with my friends."

    b) "You've apologized before and see, it happened again."

    c) "No, you aren't going to blame me. You need to control your temper."

    d) "I'm not a piece of property."

    e) "You can't love me and say and do these terrible things."

4. Say "NO" when things aren't what you want. You have a right to your opinion and feelings.

5. Suggest he talk to someone to help him learn to control his anger. Look in telephone books under "Crisis" or "Drug and Alcohol". They will know who can help. Check this site on the Internet: www.apa.org/pi/pii/teen/html or call 1-800-662-HELP.

THINGS YOU CAN DO TO HELP YOU:

1. Re-establish relations with your friends. They love you and will support you. They will be truthful, too.
2. Tell someone you trust what is happening to you…family, priest or minister, teacher or counselor, etc.
3. Keep family and friends involved in what is going on.
4. Call Families in Crisis or other agencies in the telephone book. They deal with this daily and will guide you.
5. Call Alcoholics Anonymous or Alateen or Department of Human Services. All of these will help you.
6. Call the national hotline at 1-800-799-SAFE or 1-800-422-4453.
7. Get on the Internet www.loveisnotabuse.com or www.rainn.org or www.apa.org/pi/pii/teen
8. Go to a shelter if you need protection. Crisis agencies will know where they are located. Call 1-800-399-0990.
9. Be busy with school, activities, and family so you aren't with him as much.
10. DON'T be alone with him. Take a friend with you or meet at a busy place.
11. DON'T get in the car alone with him.
12. DON'T let him in your house when you are alone.
13. Call the police to report the abuse.
14. Get a protective order against him.
15. Join a support group. Agencies will know of them.

16. Take friends with you when you break up. A suggestion would be a girl friend and a BIG guy.

17. GET OUT OF THIS RELATIONSHIP *NOW*!

18. This is your life...SAVE IT!

This is NOT what is best for YOU!.

Finally, if you've made mistakes, even serous ones, there is always another chance for you.

Failure is not falling down, but staying down and doing nothing. You must decide to do something for yourself NOW! You are in your teens, and will live to be 80 years old, so look...how far your life has to go.

Born......|Teen|......20......30......40......50......60......70......80

You can see that you have a long time ahead of you!

Now, what mistake do you need to forgive yourself for? You will live through your bad decisions! You may even become a better person because of them. Each journey starts with a single step. Forgive yourself and start that journey to a new life. You can do it. Remember, next time ask, **"Is this what's best for ME?"**

Test Your Boyfriend

Answer "yes" or "no" to the following questions:

1. _____ Does he always want you to himself?

2. _____ Does he want you to stop seeing your friends?

3. _____ Are you always the one giving in?

4. ____ Do you wish he would stop telling you what to do?

5. ____ Does he lie to you?

6. ____ Is it hard to trust him?

7. ____ Has he betrayed you before?

8. ____ Is he selfish and always wants his way?

9. ____ Do you always have to do and go where he wants?

10. ____ Do you feel smothered all the time?

11. ____ Does he think only of himself?

12. ____ Does he act like he "owns" you?

13. ____ Does he ignore your wants or needs?

14. ____ Are you afraid to tell him your real feelings?

15. ____ Does he anger easily?

16. ____ Does his anger scare you?

17. ____ Does he blame you when he gets angry?

18. ____ Has he ever slapped or hit you?

19. ____ Has he ever twisted your arm or held you down?

20. ____ Do you give-in to what he wants to avoid a fight?

21. ____ Is all your free time controlled by him?

22. ____ Does he demand things of you?

23. ____ Does he drink too much or use drugs?

24. ____ Has he ever thrown or wrecked things on purpose?

25. ____ Has he ever gotten in a fight with another guy for talking to you?

26. ____ Are you afraid he will blow up?

27. ____ Do you hide things about yourself because you know it'll make him mad?

28. ____ Does he get angry when you want to talk about things that interest you?

29. ____ Does he call you names or say you're worthless and no good?

30. ____ Is he really wonderful and apologetic after slapping or hitting you?

31. ____ Does he say he is the only one who really loves and understands you?

32. ____ Does he blame you for the bad things he does?

33. ____ Does he ignore what you say or feel?

34. ____ Is it hard to be yourself with him?

35. ____ Do you often feel up tight or have stomachaches after you're with him?

36. ____ Does he promise to change often?

37. ____ Does he often say, "It won't happen again?"

38. ____ Do you give in to things when you don't want to?

39. ____ Is he critical of what you wear, how you look, etc?

40. ____ Do you often feel that you can't do anything right?

41. ____ Is listening to you a problem for him?

42. ____ Does he make you feel bad about yourself?

43. ____ Does he make decisions for you?

44. ____ Do you feel like you are in quicksand, slipping away from who you are?

45. ____ Does he act hurt, then makes you feel guilty?

46. ____ Does he always want to know your every move?

47. ____ Does he ever say, "Don't walk away from me when I'm talking to you?"

48. _____ Does he say people are wrong and say unfair things about him?

49. _____ Do you feel when he hurts you, it is your fault?

50. _____ Are you hurt, confused and frightened?

Keep track of the number of "yes" answers. Now go back to the chapter and see what it means for you.

Annette Fuson

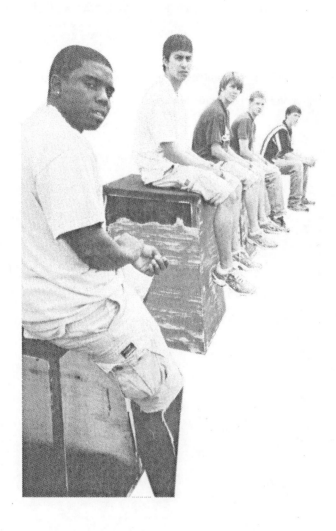

Chapter 10

Goals, Dreams and You!

Cassandra, 16, is the youngest of five children. Her two older sisters had babies and still live at home. Their house is crowded and busy. All her brothers and sisters quit school, so her parents don't expect her to continue either. Cassandra has always loved school and would like to go to college and become a teacher. Her family makes fun of her dream. She's upset and doesn't know how to cope with this. "What do I do? Do I give up my dream?"

Goals are things you want to achieve or you want to happen. They need to be **your** goals, not other peoples. Once you have your goal, then you make a road map to get there. The road map is little things that have to happen along the way to help you reach that goal.

What do you want to do with your life? Do you want a career? What do you see yourself as? A 20 year old single mother with three kids? Or a teacher, doctor, nurse, lawyer, scientist, beautician, owner of a company? The list is endless!

As an example, if your goal is to be a nurse or doctor, then your road map would be:

1. Do well in school.
2. Take math and science classes.

3. Start saving money or apply for scholarships.

4. Talk to nurses or doctors like you want to become to see if the job is like you dream it will be.

5. Be sure you like people and get along well with them.

6. Take psychology classes in college.

7. Don't plan to marry early because you'll have lots of years in school.

8. Check out colleges for your field.

9. Take care of your health; don't use drugs or alcohol.

10. Keep your goal in mind daily because you'll be in college 4 -6 years.

11. Know all the work and sacrifices will be worth it.

12. Keep a postiive attitude.

If you don't know what you want to do with your life, use these suggestions:

1. Take an aptitude test. It reveals things you are good at, skills you have.

2. Think about what things you enjoy doing, what kind of jobs use these traits.

3. Talk to a counselor for advice.

4. How much money do you want to make?

5. Go to the library and research jobs, salaries and skills needed for each job.

6. Learn how much education is needed for the job.

7. What classes do you need to take in high school to prepare you?

8. Visit people that do these jobs and actually see what they do.

How about a goal for your looks? If you're not happy with the way you look, you can do something about it.

1. Go to a professional hair designer and have your hair cut and styled. To find one, notice other peoples' hair that you like and ask who does it. After you hear one name three times, call them. Ask them how to care for your hair.

2. There are many free places to teach you about makeup. Department stores, Mary Kay and other consultants. Even a friend whose makeup you like, ask her help. Be sure to take care of your skin.

3. Clothes and wardrobe. Ask the homemaking teacher for help. Check out books for style for your figure. Read how to put clothes together. Notice girls that you admire, how they dress, then use their ideas. Look in magazines for the style that's you. If you don't have much money, go to consignment shops.

4. Health and exercise. Do you really need to lose weight or are you too thin? Don't become a diet nut! Exercise for figure problems. Again, the library can help. Eat some good nutritious foods - fruits, vegetables and lean meat.

5. Now SMILE. That will do wonderful things for your face and attitude. When you give smiles away, they keep coming back to you!

Decide on a small goal and then plan what things you have to do to reach that goal. Remember your goals must be things **you** want to happen, not someone else. This is like planning a vacation, then thinking about all the things you need to do and take with you to have a great vacation.

In setting your goals, make sure they are realistic. Don't set them so high that they are unattainable. They need to be possible, but they need to stretch you, too.

Dreams - A dream is something you hope will happen. Sometimes a dream can become a goal. Now close your eyes and see yourself at age 21, 28 and 35 years old. What do you see yourself doing? What are you doing with your life? How do you feel about yourself? Are these good feelings? Are these the things that you want to happen? At age 21, are you single or married? Can you come and go as you please? Do you have your own apartment and car? Do you have a job? Can you imagine having your own money, going away for the weekend, buying whatever you want and not having parents telling you what to do? That doesn't need to be a dream! Sound great? All of these things can happen IF you watch the choices and decisions you make along this teenage path. Set your goals now.

Are you dreaming about "the guy" and life with him? That's a nice dream too, but give yourself time for YOU. The nice guy, the house and the kids can come later. Do some things for you first, and live a little.

Don't dream to be rich and famous. Most of those people are not as happy as you think they are. Money isn't happiness. It does buy things, but it can't buy health, happiness and friends. True happiness is having family and friends that love you and give you support. Friends that stand by you and like you for yourself. Being proud of who you are, content and caring about others, these are important.

You want to do something in your life you enjoy and bring some happiness in the lives of others. Plan to do one small thing every day to give someone else a smile or pleasure. They can be people you don't even know. Compliment people, open doors for the elderly, do something unexpected for someone, take in the neighbor's garbage can, walk someone's pet, offer to run an errand - anything kind and thoughtful. You will feel so good. Be around happy, upbeat people, instead of people who complain or pull you down. Start a hobby or enter an activity each week or month that you love. Treat yourself. Take lessons in something you've always wanted to do. Make your life full and fun. Follow your dreams!

YOU - You can be anyone you want to be. You can do anything you want to do...if you work hard and are willing to pay the consequences! The consequences are sacrifices you have to make to achieve what you want.

Abraham Lincoln ran for office many times before he won. It was years before he became president. Walt Disney tried to sell his cartoons many years before they sold. Lots of famous people tried their dream and fell on their knees before they were successful.

YOU WRITE THE SCRIPT FOR YOUR LIFE! To help you see yours, get some old magazines and catalogs. Make a collage of your dreams as you see yourself now and in the future. Cut out pictures, words and sayings of things you love, things you want, things that show your goals and dreams. Cut out words or sayings that are "you." Then buy a poster board and glue them on so you can see yourself every day. Be sure and put a smiling girl on there! Now, study your collage. What does it tell you about yourself? What do you see that you had forgotten? What things can you expand? What can you do to make some of these dreams become a reality? What kind of plan do you need? Can you start the plan now?

Focus on the good in your life, not the bad. Change the bad if you can; otherwise accept it and begin to think positive. Do things you are good at and enjoy. Surround yourself with happy people, whenever you can. People you like. All these things will make you feel good about you! After all, **you are the most important person in the world**...to yourself! You deserve it!

You are a unique individual, a good person; because God doesn't make any junk! It doesn't matter how old you are, what you've done before, what kind of family you have, if you are rich or poor - you can do whatever YOU want with your life. **It is never too late to be who you want to be!**

Use the information in this book to help and guide you toward the mature woman that you know is there. If you need more information, be sure to seek out adults that can help you. There are teachers, coaches, counselors, ministers, Big Sisters, aunts, grandmothers, librarians, crisis lines, help lines, etc... Don't give up! Always remember at each step along the way, ask: **"Is this what's BEST for me?"** Hopefully, your choices each time will be the right ones! Happy journey.

Chapter 11
Questions
& Answers

The following are questions from real teenage girls.

Sincere thanks to:

Candice Arocha	Veronica Rodriquez
Reagan Greenfield	Loni King
Charlotte Hitchman	Kayla Robins
Stephanie Inskeep	Amanda Wilsterman
Emily Pope	

PERSONAL

1. Q. I want to get my navel pierced. What about it?

A. Every teen generation does things that's different. Something no one else is doing. Maybe it is a little rebelling. It seems for this generation it's piercing. Teens are piercing their navel, nose, eyebrow, tongue and lip. They need to remember that when they no longer want it, then they will have a hole or scar. A good thing about choosing your navel is the scar won't be seen like one that would be on your face. Be sure to consider how people you admire will view piercing, including boys you like. In some groups it is accepted. Other groups will think you are wild or weird. Will you be wearing clothes that would be uncomfortable or to show off your naval? Watch that you don't choose clothes that make you look like a slut. It would be great if you could discuss this with your parents and get their view before you choose what to do.

2. Q. Most of my friends have some type of tattoo, but my Mom is freaking! What can I do?

A. This may be another teenage fad, like piercing. The difference is a tattoo is *permanent*. Before you decide what to do, there are some things to think through carefully. 1. You may want something small like a flower or a heart instead of something large that would be hard to cover up. (As you get older, you may regret the tattoo.) 2. Think of putting it somewhere inconspicuous, like your breast or buttock. If you put it on your ankle, hand or arm and then you get a professional job, it might not fit the image that you then want to portray.3. What will the people you admire think? (Some people view tattoos as rebellion.) 4. How might you feel about it when you are 25 years old? 5. It is best NOT to have a guy's name or initials done. Your chances of breaking up are 99% and you'd be stuck with the tattoo forever. 6. Have you discussed this with your parents? You are very smart to think it through instead of being impulsive.

3. Q. I hear rumors on what causes zits and what doesn't. What is the truth?

A. A great question. Even dermatologists disagree. The trouble is there are several answers and no one knows what might cause yours. Be sure to clean your face. Use a cleanser for your skin type. (Dry, combination, oily, sensitive.) Try to get eight hours of sleep. Drink lots of water. Cut out Cokes or any drink that says cola in it. Cut out chocolate and see if it gets better. Some people have allergies to certain things that cause breakouts. Cut back on sweets and try to eat some fruits and vegetables. If you are oily, choose oil free make up. Start with those suggestions and see if you clear up. Many teen breakouts are due to hormones. That is why they are worse just before your period. When you are a teenager you have more pimples due to body changes. You have no control over these things. Heredity plays a part, too. Some people never have a problem because of that; other's skin are terrible. There are new and great medications to help if you have terrible skin problems. See a doctor that others recommend. The good news is your skin usually becomes clear as you reach 18-20 years old, so hang in there.

4. Q. Is there anything wrong in using over the counter medications for pimples?

A. Yes and no. Use them for a short time to see if they help. Some of them will dry you out, turn you red or cause a rash. Use caution. Products that have benzyl peroxide will be helpful. A few old fashion ideas to help dry up a pimple while you sleep are: a clay mask, a dab of toothpaste (like regular CREST) or yeast paste (mix water with dry yeast). Put it ONLY ON THE PIMPLE and NOT every night.

5. Q. What is the difference between acne and pimples?

A. Acne is usually hereditary. They look like large purplish bumps and never come to a head or change much. They are more often on boys because of their hormone, testosterone. Pimples are usually on all teenagers' faces. They are small red bumps. Sometimes they develop a white pus like head. You should not SQUEEZE them. That spreads them and makes scars. See questions above for help.

6. Q. Why do teenagers break out more when they are stressed?

A. Stress is another cause of breakouts for everyone. Many causes of pimples are internal. Stress is one of them. Sorry that there is no magic answer to handle stress. The best answer is to try to forget the things over which you have no control. Another hint is to choose your battles. That means if it is really important to you, then work at solving it or talking out a solution - but let the rest go. No one can cause you stress - you choose to have it.

7. Q. When should you start wearing make-up and what type should you wear?

A. Usually girls wear makeup when their skin begins to change and they develop pimples or some breakouts. This is about 13-14 years old. It all depends on your maturity. Before that, the skin is smooth and young looking and make up is not needed. You choose the type depending on your skin type. The skin types are: dry, combination, normal, oily and sensitive. Dry skin needs makeup that is oil based because dry skin needs extra moisture. Combination skin needs water based makeup because this person has more than one type of skin type on her face. Normal skin can wear either one. Oily skin needs oil free makeup and sensitive skin must figure out what causes the problem and use make up especially for that situation. Choosing a color is VERY important. It is best to match the color of your neck so you won't have a make up line. When you notice the time of year that you are lighter, wear the light color on you cheeks and chin and darker color above that. That gives you more color in the center of your face.

8. Q. How do I choose eyeshadow, blush and lip colors? How do I know which colors are best for me?

A. This is important. First, the blush and lip color should be in the same color family. Either pinks, peaches, browns, neutrals, reds or berries. When using eye colors to go with the blush and lip color, choose warm or cool colors.

WARM		COOL	
Blush and Lip	**Eye**	**Blush & Lip**	**Eye**
Peach, Brown	Browns, Teal	Pink, Red	Grey, White
Neutral, Rust	Ginger, Honey	Rose	Taupe
Red orange	Bronze, Olive	Berries	Plum, Maroon

To decide which colors are best for you, notice what colors you get your most compliments. You will come alive in your best colors.

9. Q. In the winter, how can I keep from drying out without using lotion and getting oily?

A. You have found there is a lot to know about skin problems. The lotions made for your face are called moisturizers. Hand lotion and body lotions are specially made for those parts of the body and usually do not do well on the face. There are many types of moisturizers. You need an oil free one on the part of your face that tends to get oily. You may need another type for your cheeks. Some moisturizers are heavy for drier skin and some are lighter. There are many make up companies that give free makeovers and consultations. Go to several and you will find one you trust. Never take credit cards or money with you, because you will not want to be pressured to buy anything until you wear it all day.

10. Q. Is it true that shaving your legs before age 16 causes you to have a hairy body?

A. NO! Shaving doesn't cause a hairy body. After you start to shave your legs or underarms then you need to shave on a regular basis. The hair end is now blunt and shows more. If your hair on your legs are dark and it bothers you, then you need to shave them regularly even at age 13. Too often, mothers forbid girls from shaving, but your mother doesn't have to take the teasing from others like you do. If, however, your hair is very light, don't shave until you really need to do it. Once you start, there is no stopping.

11. Q. I have a mustache, help!

A. Don't fret. There is help for your problem. Don't shave it. Go to the drug department and find a depilatory for the FACE. Follow the directions, but don't leave it on as long as it says the first time. The hair will wash away. If your face turns red, take a Tums or antacid tablet before you do it next time. It must be re-applied every few weeks. If that doesn't appeal to you, your hair stylist can use a wax treatment and remove it. Again, these are temporary. For permanent removal, you need electrolysis. Another idea is to bleach it so it doesn't show as much. Good luck.

12. Q. Should you keep a calendar for your periods?

A. YES. Not only so you can keep track when it happens, but after a few months you should be able to determine when you will start the next month. That is the important thing to know. Then you can be prepared. Also, you can plan activities around those days, if you need to. You can be sure to have cramp medication with you, too.

13. Q. What is the best way to avoid cramps or deal with them?

A. There may not be a way to avoid cramps. It depends on the cause. Some girls have very severe cramps because of special problems. These girls have special needs and usually need help from their doctor. Normal cramps before your period starts are caused by your hormone level dropping. This causes the muscles in the uterus to work and start sloughing the lining. There is medicine on the market for these cramps. Or use aspirin or some other type pain reliever during this time of the month. Regular exercise and rest can help minimize the cramps. Go about your regular activities and have fun. That will help keep your mind off the problem. If the cramps are unbearable, see your doctor for help.

14. Q. How can I keep from being sad or mad when I have my period?

A. What you are experiencing is PMS. These are normal feelings. There is over the counter medication you can get. Try Pamprin, Naproxen or Midol. The best thing you can do is to focus on other things - your friends, sports, activities - be active and involved and you will forget about it. If you are real bad, see your doctor.

15. Q. I am fair skinned and people make fun of me. They say, "You are so white!" "You should get a tan." This bothers me. I'm thinking about going to a tanning salon. What should I do?

A. If your skin is very smooth, those people may be jealous. Making fun of you is their way of hurting you to make themselves feel good. There is evidence that the sun and tanning salons are dangerous for your skin. You definitely want to protect your face from getting future wrinkles. Tanning is also time consuming and costs money. Have you tried the sunless tan products on the market? They work well, on legs especially, but they can be used on the body, too. You should really try to shrug off those comments and be happy with your looks.

16. Q. Why do girls feel they have to be thin? Especially if we are happy with our bodies.

A. What insight you have for your age! Girls seem to be obsessed with being thin. The real trouble comes when they want to be **too** thin. That is unhealthy. Teen bodies are growing and developing, therefore, they need good nutrition. It is much healthier to accept the body you have until you are through your teens. The exception to that is if you are very over weight. That is a problem that needs a doctor's care. Being happy with your body is far more important than being thin. Girls should not look at weight charts because most girls carry weight in their hips or legs but have a nice waist. Therefore, they don't **look** heavy. Other's have large bones, so they will weigh heavy, but not look that way. You should ask an adult that you trust for an assessment of your weight. Sadly, our society causes the weight phobia. Teens should be focused on activities, school and friends - not weight. They should try to enjoy their life. Teens have enough to worry about, don't add one more worry. Hats off to you!

17. Q. I have a friend who never eats during the day. This has been going on for over a year. Should I be concerned about her?

A. Yes! It seems you are concerned and for good reason. She is one of those girls in the above question. It is very unhealthy for teens to stop eating. All their body systems get messed up. Even their periods stop. Hopefully, it is not too late to help her. Talk to a school counselor or a trusted teacher. They can approach her parents and see that she gets help. This is not squealing on her, it is helping save her life. You show compassion and caring.

18. Q. Can I take over the counter medication to curb my appetite?

A. You can, but you shouldn't. If you have a sincere weight problem, see your doctor for a good diet for your situation. Otherwise, cut out colas and sweets. Then exercise with friends. That is safer than diet pills.

19. Q. I do not like my hair, it's very curly. I wish it were straight. I want to have it straightened, but Mom says those products will ruin my hair. Is this true?

A. You have curly hair and wish it were straight. Probably, your good friend has straight hair and wishes it were curly. There is a lesson here. Seriously, it is funny how we all wish for something else. To answer your question, yes, those products could ruin your hair - if not applied correctly. There is nothing you can do to make your hair straight, permanently. You could use a conditioner and it will soften your curls. You might try large rollers or have a hair stylist show you how to use a straightening iron. The very best answer is to accept your hair and try different styles, clips, bows, etc and forget the trouble - because it won't stay straight.

20. Q. How can I keep my hair from getting frizzy?

A.For information on products, have a professional help you. Go to a store that sells hair supplies or talk to your stylist. It depends on your hair type as to what to use. Many conditioners will help. Be sure not to brush your hair while it is still wet. Don't use nylon brushes. Sometimes frizzies are caused from hair being too dry. Have a professional help you.

21. Q. What can I do to not be so shy?

A. Wanting to do something is the first step. Quit thinking about yourself so much. Concentrate on others instead. Talk to them about things they like. Compliment others when you notice something good they did. Say "hi" to people that you know. SMILE. Act happy, not scared. Listen to what is happening in your friends' lives, then comment later about those happenings. Take a drama class or try out for a part in a play. All these ideas will make people like you, too. You might read some books about shyness, too. Remember, think of others. Good luck.

22. Q. Why don't guys have PMS?

A. Interesting question. Guys don't have PMS because they don't have periods. PMS is hormonal. In a way, it is too bad, because if guys had it, they would understand girls better.

23. Q. Why are girls so impatient for love?

A. You are very observant. It does seem that love is all girls think about at times. It probably starts when girls are very young. They read fairy tales about the princess and prince living happily ever after and they dream of being that princess. Television shows and romantic novels also play up "love" to make the girl desire it for herself. Love is wonderful, but it takes maturity to find it and know it. It also grows over time. Teenagers usually are in love with love - not the person. Your teen years are when you meet many personalities to see what you like and dislike in people. In that way, you are forming what you "love" in a guy. Hopefully, you will find it one day. Don't be in a hurry. It will come.

BOYS

24. Q. Do guys prefer a sporty girl or a girly girl?

A. Every guy is different, like girls are different. Some will prefer sporty, others girly or musical or intellectual, etc. Usually the two of you have common interests. It is important to do things you like and dress in your **own** style. Then when "the guy" sees you and likes you, you aren't fake.

25. Q. How do you get a guy to notice you or like you?

A. To get the guy to notice you, you need an act of magic! You can't make the guy notice you or like you, but you can do things to make guys in general notice you. Develop your own style. What you like to wear and do. Be clean. Be fun and willing to try new things. Act natural. SMILE and be friendly. Too often when girls like a guy, they act like they **don't** like him. They ignore him or snub him. Guys see you act that way and think that they don't have a chance, so you never get together. TALK to him. He needs to know that you are at least friendly. Say "hi" when you see him. Pretend he is a girl you'd like to be friends with and treat him that way. The rest will come. At the least you'll have a new friend that's a boy.

26. Q. How do you know if a guy likes you?

A. Sometimes you never know! Usually you catch him watching you. His friends tease him in front of you. If he is a young teen, he'll show-off when you are around. If he is older and more experienced, he will talk to you and give you lots of attention. He'll ask you out. Interestingly, girls seldom like the boys that like them. But NEVER treat guys rudely, because as he matures, he may become the one you want!

27. Q. How do you kiss a boy?

A. That is a great question. We are not born knowing everything, we have to learn. Kissing a guy is not hard. Relax your lips. Do NOT pucker-up. Don't hold your lips tightly together. You will usually know when he is going to kiss you. (Unless it is his first time and he'll just quickly give you a peck.) He will tilt his head to one side so you won't bump noses or glasses. You gently turn your head the other way. When your lips meet, you can push against him with your mouth or relax. You can gently move your mouth around or even touch tongues. This is your choice. If he tries to put his tongue in your mouth and you don't want him to, then put your lips together. As you kiss more guys, you'll get better and know what kind of kiss you prefer. Relax and enjoy!

28. Q. When do you know to kiss a guy?

A. You will probably just know. He looks at you, you are usually alone, he is quiet and you just feel "it" is going to happen. You, of course, must quit talking and be quiet, too. Guys usually take the lead here when you begin dating. Later, you kiss him when you feel like it.

117

Annette Fuson

29. Q. Why do guys show off and do dumb things?

A. Guys like to believe they have it together, but they don't. At least not for a while. Girls are new territory for them and they can't figure girls out. Therefore, they don't know what to do when they are around you. So...they show off and do dumb things. They hit and push each other. They run and jump to hit a light or ceiling. They say stupid things. It is like they come unwound and fall apart. Then you notice them and start to giggle, so the boys show off more. It is nervousness and inexperience showing.

30. Q. Why do boys say nasty things to girls or use dirty language?

A. Sometimes it is a way to show off to the girls and to other guys. They think it makes them look macho or grown-up. It doesn't. Maybe they hear the language all the time and think they are suppose to use it. If you don't like it, then it is important to tell them or act like it offends you. They may do it to see how you react. Like telling dirty jokes. They want to see what you'll do. Say, "I don't like being called names" or "I'd rather you wouldn't say that." Boys will take their cue from what you do.

31. Q. Why do boys grab at girls' breasts or butts?

A. To see if they can get away with it. To see what you'll do. Because they can be crude. This is another dumb thing they do when they are young. Maybe they are trying to see what girls feel like. BUT, it is your body, protect it! DON'T laugh. Then they will think you enjoy it and they will do it more.

32. Q. Why do I need to go on team dates before I go on a "real" date?

A. You team date when you are young so you can learn about boys in general. You are more relaxed in a group. You can do fun things and learn about personalities that you like and dislike. People will react differently to situations. You learn about yourself, too. It is a time of learning and experimenting on safe ground because there are lots of other people around. You aren't put in awkward situations and have to get out of them all by yourself. You can see how other girls handle boys, too. All this is important to help you gain confidence dealing with people. You can go on a "real" date when you feel ready and your parents agree. It would depend on the maturity of the girl, but generally 16 years or older. Don't rush it.

33. Q. How do you tell a guy that you don't want to go out with him without hurting his feelings?

A. It is good that you are sensitive to his feelings. Just say you're busy. Keep saying it and he will get the message. Don't say "I'm sorry, I'd love to", because then he'll keep asking you. You could say, "I'm interested in someone else" or "I'm in too many activities and don't have the time." When all else fails say, "I enjoy your friendship and I want to keep it that way." Be sure you have a good reason for not going out with him. Never judge on looks or hearsay from others about a person. You may miss a great friendship by refusing. Every date doesn't have to be you having passion for the guy. Girls need to go out with LOTS of guys in order to see what kind of guys' personalities that they like. Besides, many people have met the "special one" while being on a date with someone else.

34. Q. How do you break up with a guy in a polite way?

A. You may not be able to do it politely. If he likes you a lot, no matter what you say or do, he'll be hurt. Put yourself in his shoes, how would you feel? Be kind. You start by not being so available to go places or talk on the phone. Go out with your friends more. Slowly you are pulling away. This will help prepare him when you finally get to talk about breaking up. Things you can say are: "We don't have as much time for each other." "Things haven't been the same." "We are both so busy." "My mother says that we're seeing too much of each other." "We're too young and need to go with others." Be gentle and tell him how you feel. You may want to go with him again, so leave the relationship as friends.

35. Q. My boyfriend is not very talkative. Some people say he is shy or is it that he is not really into our relationship?

A. It could be many reasons. He may be just a quiet person or a thinker, not a talker. He may not know what to talk about. Many guys are afraid to talk to girls. They are afraid of saying something dumb or being laughed at. He may really like you, so you need to help him become more comfortable. Be yourself and be honest. Talk about things he can relate to: school, sports, latest music, likes and dislikes, goals and dreams. Ask him questions that are easy, like some of his favorite vacations, books, movies. Why he liked them and what he did that he enjoyed. Laugh together and do things you both enjoy. Boys, no matter what their age, need help talking to girls. But especially when they are new in a relationship. Good luck. It will be worth it. Remember, girls are the talkers, not the guys.

36. Q. My ex-boyfriend was so nice to my parents and friends, but when we were alone he was pushy sexually. He tried to pressure me to do things I didn't want to do. I kept telling him "no" thinking he would respect me, but he got mad instead. I don't understand.

A. This seems to be very common in young relationships. Sometimes boys think they have to try stuff because their friends tell them that they do things. Some boys try things to see what kind of girl you are. They may do it to experiment, at your expense. You were wise to stick to what you believe and wanted to do. It is your body, not his. Don't let him take advantage of your innocence. When a boy truly cares about you, he wants you to be happy and respects your wishes. Often times, guys are one personality to parents or friends and a completely different person when alone, as you've found. You must be the judge of what is right for you - not parents or friends. Congratulations on your good judgement.

37. Q.   At age 16, guys tend to be moving faster in a relationship than girls would like them to. How can girls get them to cool it?

A. As in the answer above - many guys will go as far as you will let them. Girls need to be the one to keep control over what happens. You need to think ahead. What do you feel is right and wrong for you. Each person decides this for herself. Be honest and tell the boy how you feel, such as, "I like you, but we're going too fast for me." "I'm not ready for that." "I want to do things with our friends." There are many suggestions to help you in chapter 6 and chapter 7.

38. Q.   How far should you go with a guy before he thinks you are leading him on to sex?

A. A good question. It may depend on the boy. Some boys may try things when you did nothing to lead them on. Usually you can hug and kiss, French kiss or maybe he can feel your body on top of your clothes. After that, what you let him do would be leading him on. If you let him feel your skin, unbutton, unzip or take off clothes…that would be too far. Boys decide what to do by what girls let them do. They take their cues from you. Some girls dress so sexy, or wear no bra or underwear, then wonder why the guy tries something. You might have made him think that you wanted him to do something by how you dressed. You need to be in control and realize what you are doing. Chapters 7 and 8 can help you understand this more.

39. Q. What do guys want to see girls wear: tight clothes or not?

A. Truthfully, tight clothes - but for all the wrong reasons. Guys like to look at girls' bodies. Girls' bodies are different and attractive and by just looking, get guys excited. You need to realize though, when you dress in tight clothes that you are "advertising" and guys might think you want them to touch you or make comments. They enjoy looking, but they don't want their girlfriends wearing tight clothes around others. Therefore, you can never go wrong wearing clothes that fit, but you can get in trouble wearing tight clothes.

40. Q. What does "dress like a slut or ho'" mean? Why is it wrong?

A. This is a hard question, but a good one. The fashion magazines, music groups and television programs show all these outfits that show off the body. The people are famous and attractive, so, of course, girls copy the looks. They do it innocently, thinking they look attractive, too. A "slut" or "ho" is a girl who dresses provocatively to arouse the boy and make him want sex with her. Most girls who dress this way are really innocent and don't realize what they are advertising. Dressing slutty is when the clothes are really tight, low cut and short. They show lots of skin and they don't wear a bra. A slut also wears way too much make up. You can figure out, now, why it is wrong - if that's not what you want to portray to the world then you are giving a wrong and bad impression. You can be fashionable and dress like you want by toning it down a little and making sure the clothes aren't skin tight.

41. Q. Why is it wrong to have sex with several guys?

A. The biggest reason is the huge damage that is done to your confidence and self-esteem. You begin to feel used and no good because the guys don't respect you. They just use you for their pleasure and drop you. The more guys you have sex with, the greater chance of STD, AIDS or pregnancy. Also, your reputation goes down the tubes. Your body is in the developing stage so it is dangerous to have sex with many guys. If you've been promiscuous, as you get older, there is a greater chance of cervical cancer. Chapter 9 gives hope to get out of this situation. Enjoy boys as friends. There will be plenty of time later to decide on sexual relationships. Work on taking care of yourself, your body, your friendships and your future and don't concern yourself with only sex right now.

PARENTS

42. Q. Why are parents so strict about boys and dating?

A. Believe it or not, parents love you and worry about you. They generally trust you, but they may not trust the boy. They are so concerned that you will make some choices that will hurt you and your future. They want you to achieve your goals and be happy. If you enter into a sexual relationship, you can get pregnant and your future falls apart. Parents worry about the boy being involved in drugs and alcohol. Another worry is his driving. They want you to be prepared for all kinds of choices when it involves boys, but they have little control over you, once you are dating. Think before you act. It is your future. Be trustworthy and make them proud.

43. Q. Why are parents more protective of their daughters than their sons?

A. Part of your answer is above. They are afraid of all the things that can happen to daughters, including rape. The percentage of bad things happening to girls is much higher than what happens to boys. Boys can get involved in drugs and alcohol, too, but not pregnancy and rape. Unwanted pregnancy or getting raped are terrible things that happen to girls that affect their emotions deeply and forever. Parents desperately want what is best for their sons and daughters. They worry, though, because they can't be there to help you. Parents may think boys can handle themselves because they are stronger. That may or may not be true, but that may be their thinking. Teenagers are impulsive and don't think anything will ever happen to them. Parents know better, so they worry and are therefore more protective of their daughters.

44. Q. Why do parents treat you like a 5-year-old?

A. That is a question from every girl. You feel that they think you are still a little girl. It is true that your dad doesn't want you to ever grow up. He doesn't like to face that you'll like another guy when he has always been the guy in your life. You must convince your parents that you can take care of yourself. That you can make good decisions, be trustworthy and can drive safely. Share small things with them so they feel they are a part of your life and can see you use your head. Be on time, go where you say you will, introduce your friends to them. Try your best in school. Doing these things will show them you are maturing and you're not a child. They need reassurance. Tell them how you feel without yelling and screaming. Discuss things with them so they can see your good thinking. Maybe ask, "How can I learn things if you never let me try?" Showing them you are not a child will help. Good luck.

45. Q. Mothers are so nosey, sometimes. I hate that. What can I do about it?

A. Yes, they are! There are three reasons mothers may be nosey. They are just interested, a nib-nose or want to calm their fears that everything is all right. Figure out your mother's reason.

Is she that way with everyone? Have you ever given her reason to not trust you? Is she just a person who worries a lot? There are some things you can try so it won't be such a problem. Tell her things that are not important to you. Examples: "Shanda was on the phone. She's worried about a test." "They had the best music at the party!" "At school today, the funniest thing happened..." When you share, even little things with her, she feels she is a part of your life. She knows some things that are happening to you. When you choose to share information before she asks, then you are deciding what to tell her. Usually, mothers are afraid that you are getting involved in dangerous situations. They worry that maybe you can't handle yourself. You might also talk to her about a television show, article in a magazine or situation that happened to a teen. Tell her your ideas and viewpoint on what the girl should have done or what you would have done to avoid the problem. These ideas will reassure your mother and hopefully, get her off your back.

46. Q. My parents drive me crazy worrying about me driving at night. I'm a good driver, so why don't they trust me?

A. It isn't that they don't trust you. They know the statistics for teenage drivers and they don't want you to be one of them. Statistically, teens have more fatal accidents than any other age group. One reason is inexperience, but for each teenager riding with the teen driver, the percentage goes up. If a teenage boy is in the car, it doubles. That is scary! When teens ride together, they are having fun, laughing and talking, so it is harder to concentrate on driving. Teens are naturally impulsive and tend not to think things through. Parents also worry about alcohol entering into the picture. Not you, necessarily, but another drunk driver. If you feel uneasy about some situations or some people riding in your car, say "NO!" You can always blame your parents - "My dad won't let me have more than two ride with me." "I'm sorry, I forgot I have to be home early." "I feel sick and need to go home." As you show more maturity driving, your parents will relax. Earn their trust and save *your* life.

47. Q. My parents are divorced, but they still go on dates together. What's the deal? Other parents don't do that.

A. Everyone is different. Each situation is different. Your parents must be friends or are trying to be, for your sake. This way, they can discuss things involving their children. Maybe they just enjoy each other's company. If they aren't yelling and fighting then consider yourself lucky. So many parents put their kids in the middle. It is too bad more parents don't do what yours are doing.

48. Q. I'm 15 years old and was invited to a party. My mother called to see if the parents were going to be there. They said yes. When I got there, the parents served us beer and then left! I didn't know what to do, I was so scared.

A. What a terrible spot for you. You are to be commended for not getting upset about your mother calling their parents. If you haven't told your mother, do it now. Your openness and honesty will pay off. It is almost impossible to imagine parents doing this. When the parents served beer to underage teens, they were breaking the law and could be arrested. When you find yourself in these spots, it is hard to say no. Something you could do is pretend you are ill and call your parents to come after you. Besides, you probably felt ill. Serving beer is inexcusable, but leaving teenagers alone brings a whole new world of problems. Keep the lines of communication open with your mother. She is there to help you through these hard times. By doing this, you are building trust and that is so important of you. Congratulations on your forthrightness.

GENERAL

49. Q. What is the best way to confront a friend who is doing something that you know is wrong?

A. Honestly with straight forwardness. If she is a friend, you should be able to talk to her. Is this something she knows is wrong or do you have different values on this issue? You could say, "Have you thought about what you're doing?" "Are you sure this is what you want to do?" "Do you want to talk about this?" These questions will give you and her a chance to discuss it further, before she makes a mistake. Remember, though, it is her choice.

131

50. Q. You and your closest friends all have boyfriends and you spend most of your time with them. What is the best way to make sure your friendships don't suffer?

A. What a mature and compassionate question. When friends get boyfriends, usually the friendship suffers some. Some boyfriends want you all to themselves. Boyfriends will come and go, but girlfriends are for life. MAKE time each week to get together with your girlfriends. Maybe make a certain day to do something - like every Tuesday. Be sure to continue to call or email them. Tell the boyfriend that you **both** need time to spend with friends. It is not healthy for a boyfriend and girlfriend to ALWAYS be together and exclude others. You might even double date. Explain to your girlfriends what you want to do and why and brainstorm ideas to get together, such as having a slumber party once a month. Everyone needs to make an effort to keep the friendship alive.

51. Q. How do you deal with an old friend who completely dislikes you, but you don't dislike her?

A. What caused the sudden change of attitude in your old friend? Is she jealous? Did you win an honor? Is she having problems at home? "Completely dislikes" is pretty strong. Do you really want to continue this so-called friendship one-sided? If so, cool it some. Say "hi", but don't force yourself on her. Stay away from her and go about your other friendships. She may just need time to re-evaluate things. If she doesn't come around, move on with your life.

52. Q. How do you approach someone who is gossiping untruthfully?

A. Be sure you have all the facts before confronting her. Go to her with someone who heard the gossip or heard her. You need proof or it gets no where. Then, as calmly as possible, say, "Why would you say those things?" "What do you have to gain?" Give her an out - "I'm sure what I'm hearing isn't true." "What really happened?" or "I thought we were friends, why would you say these things to hurt me?" She needs to hear how you feel. Sometimes these things get out of control and people regret what they've done. Give her a chance to come clean. Maybe she isn't worth the effort and you need to just go on with your life.

53. Q. Does life get better or worse?

A. Life is what YOU make it. It is really in your attitude. If you are positive, make plans and set goals, then life gets better. If instead, you are negative and always complaining, life gets worse. If you are always thinking of yourself, life becomes shallow. Open your eyes to others. Be aware of what is going on around you. Some child could use a "big sister" or an elderly neighbor could use a visit or an errand run for them. Volunteer in a community project or at a hospital. Doing these kinds of things will make life seem good because you are doing something for others. Having things and money won't make you happy. It is how you feel inside about yourself that's important in life. Then life is good. Remember, "If it is to be, it is up to me."

54. Q. Why would God put us on this earth to deal with so much tragedy, then we have to get up the next day and go on?

A. What a powerful question. We really won't know the true answer until we can ask Him. Many people believe that things happen for reasons, even truly BAD things. Often, lots of good comes out of bad. We have to have faith and trust. Tragedy can strengthen us and make us a stronger person. As a teenager, all this probably seems so trite, but it is very true. Just look at the 9/11 tragedy and the enormous amount of good that came about, nation wide. Look at the strength so many of those people that survived had. We cannot judge. We just need to take one step at a time and go on. As you age and mature, many of these questions will have answers that you will finally understand.

55. Q. Why did God make different cultures and races?

A. Probably so things wouldn't be so boring. All the differences make life interesting. Yes, differences can cause problems - but differences can also cause challenges. Cultures, races and religions give us a wide range of ideas on which to focus. Besides, then we have all that information, knowledge and fun to use as part of our life!

56. Q. Do most people achieve their goals in their life?

A. Probably not all of them, but who knows? Hopefully, people have goals in their lives. Many people achieve them because we see evidence of it. Here is where your positive or negative attitude shows again. The people who do achieve their goals really believe they will achieve them. What matters is that you plan to make it to the goal. You do all the things that you need to, in order to get there. Then if you don't reach your "moon", you'll still end up among the "stars". What that means is, you will have done more than you would have had you not tried. You are also closer to your goal even if you don't reach it. What are your goals and what plans have you made to reach them? It is YOUR life and your responsibility.

Annette Fuson

GO FOR IT!!!

About the Author

Annette Fuson

Annette Fuson has been teaching teenage girls for over twenty years in areas that affected them as they went through the troubling teens. The classes and discussions were lively and positive. The girls needed information, ideas, encouragement and sensible answers to what was bothering them: handling emotions, building boy and girl friendships, boys lines and pressures, getting out of bad situations, understanding sex, and building goals.

She used this knowledge and experience to develop *Straight Talk for Teenage Girls*. Her B. A. and M.A. degrees are from Ball State University in Muncie, Indiana. She now resides in Belton, Texas. She is married and has one daughter and one granddaughter.

Author Information

Education

Ball State University, Muncie, Indiana

-B.A. degree - science, home economics and physical education

-M.A. degree - education management

Employment

Teacher Public Schools - 25 years

-Central Dauphin High School, Harrisburg, Pennsylvania

-New Cumberland Schools, Pennsylvania

-Harrison Township Schools, Indiana

-Muncie Community Schools, Indiana

Central Texas College - 8 years

Personal Business

Mary Kay Cosmetics - 20 years

Professional Consultant for businesses

Published Works

Inter-personal Relations curriculum for Central Texas College (used world wide on Army posts)

Printed in the United States
695500001B